ARTHUR RANSO

Afloat in Lakeland

by W.R. Mitchell

GREAT NORTHERN

Great Northern Books
PO Box 213, Ilkley, LS29 9WS
www.greatnorthernbooks.co.uk

ISBN: 978-0-9928193-3-0

Design and layout: David Burrill

CIP Data
A catalogue for this book is available from
the British Library

ACKNOWLEDGEMENTS

The author is especially grateful to the help afforded
by Brotherton Library at the University of Leeds; the
Arthur Ransome Society for the representations of
Ransome's drawings; and by the Museum of
Lakeland Life and Industry at Kendal.

My thanks are also extended to Helen Lupton,
whose late husband was a nephew of Ransome, and
Anne Read, an old friend who provided an
introduction to the Brotherton Library as a former
member of staff. My son, David, was a cheerful
chauffeur for an ageing Dad when I made special
visits to Ransome's favourite Lakeland haunts.

Photos by the author or from his collection (except
where otherwise credited)

Cover Images

Front:
Portrait of Arthur Ransome
(Brotherton Library, University of Leeds)
Lake Windermere

Back:
Gondola on Windermere

"Sail Ho! It's her," shouted Susan. From the northern entrance of the bay, beyond the long island, it was possible to see far up the lake, a long blue sheet of water stretching away into bigger hills than those which rose from the wooded banks of the southern part. Little over a mile away, a small white sail was moving rapidly towards a promontory on the western shore. In a moment or two it disappeared.

From part of a taped message from *Swallows and Amazons* the author noted years ago at the National Park Centre at Brockhole, on the shores of Windermere.

CONTENTS

Coniston Water, with Coniston Old Hall prominent by the shore of the lake.

An Introduction

Arthur Ransome, famous the world over as an author of children's adventure stories, made his name with *Swallows and Amazons*, which he set in his beloved English Lake District. What drew a Leeds lad to Lakeland? Arthur, born during the last phase of the Victorian Age, was the son of Cyril Ransome, an academic whose spare-time passion was angling. He and his family spent three summer months on vacation at the hamlet of High Nibthwaite, near the outflow of Coniston Water.

A typical, greystone Lakeland settlement, Nibthwaite huddles for shelter from northern winds under the steep sides of Brockbarrow.

In the 17th and 18th centuries, the place was industrialised, being a trans-shipment point for cargoes of ore from the Coniston mines to smelters elsewhere. The quay is still recognisable as such. Storage barns were used until new forms of transport and a decline in mining led to the area being bypassed.

As a boy, Arthur Ransome venerated the lake. On each visit, he went through a "special rite". Running across a field, he would crouch on the stone quay in order to dip a hand into the water. The swirling water marked what he considered to be his homecoming.

Not all his memories of Coniston Water were happy. When he and his father were boating on Coniston Water, father tested a theory that you need not learn to swim; it came naturally. He tossed Arthur overboard. Then, realising his mistake as the lad struggled with flailing arms, he yanked him back into the boat. Ironically, Coniston Water would lead to Cyril's death. As he returned from a fishing expedition, he had an accident that led to a protracted, painful leg infection and amputation.

Ransome's literary ambitions dated from an early age. Born on 18 January, 1884, Arthur had listened attentively as mother read aloud passages from such classics as *Robinson Crusoe* and *Treasure Island*. He experimented with various literary forms but was in his forties when success came, impulsively, with the writing of *Swallows and Amazons*, a children's adventure story published in 1930. In what would prove to be his most famous book, he blended childhood fantasies with real-life experiences. Action took place on sailing boats. Ransome was thus able to avoid sedentary situations.

The fictional crew-members of *Swallow* – John, Titty, Susan, Roger – were based on the children of Ernest Altounyan, an Armenian-Syrian doctor who had married Dora, a daughter of the much respected W G Collingwood. He had a lake view from Lanehead, his imposing home. In his story of the adventures of Swallows and Amazons, Ransome solved the problem of an all-girl crew of *Swallow* by giving Taqui Altounyan, the eldest of the family, a leading role as Captain John.

When the Altounyans had their long summer vacation based on Lanehead, two small but lusty sea-going boats were purchased by Ernest, their father. He and, to a lesser extent, Arthur Ransome instructed the children in the skills of sailing. When the children were about to return with their parents to the family home in Syria, they presented Ransome with a pair of red Turkish slippers. Impulsively, he responded to their generosity by writing *Swallows and Amazons* and dedicating the book to them. On publication, the first copy was posted to their Syrian home.

Big, bluff, virtually bald but heavily moustached, Arthur Ransome was touchy throughout his life. He also had moody spells, pondering on his writing ambitions, a failed first marriage and the course his life was taking. He remained a child at heart, as is evident when reading *Swallows and Amazons* and the eleven successive books, relating to children – adventurous children who never aged and sailed and camped in romantic places with exciting consequences.

Ted Scott, who edited the *Guardian* in Ransome's day, had a fancy to enrol Arthur as a permanent member of the editorial staff. This was not to be, though Arthur found pleasure in contributing a regular angling feature. Scott mentioned to a fellow journalist that Ransome had "some stupid notion of a personal career." He was referring to his literary ambitions, which were realised when he became a writer of highly popular children's books. When *Swallows and Amazons* was published in 1930, the *Guardian* review concluded that "Mr Ransome's book has the magical power that Lewis Carroll had of being the child in terms of himself. He never talks down; never finds it necessary to be patronising or sentimental…"

I never met Arthur Ransome, but journalistically our Lakeland lives overlapped. Arthur had returned to the Lakes in the 1940s. From the late 1950s to the 1980s I kept a journalistic finger on the pulse of everyday life as Editor of *Cumbria* magazine. Like Arthur, I had a special regard for Coniston Water, its lonely fells and vast tracts of deciduous woodland. I had camped in such a setting with the Boy Scouts. On a hot day, I helped to skin rabbits caught when local farm lads went ferreting. I was under siege from hungry wasps. I toured Lakeland in a pre-war Ford car that was afflicted by piston slap and tappet-rattle. It was no worse than Trojan, the name of Ransome's bone-shaking vehicle.

He had quit England – and his first marriage – for Russia, intending to write up a collection of folk tales. Caught up in the social and political upset of the Revolution in the autumn of 1917, Arthur switched to journalism, reporting first for the *Daily News* and then for the *Manchester Guardian*. His friendship with Bolshevik leaders led to him falling in love, and subsequently marrying Evgenia, who had been Trotsky's secretary. They lived in Russia throughout the Great War, then moved to Estonia where, over several years, Ransome cruised on the Baltic in his boat *Racundra*.

Obtaining a divorce from his wife Ivy in 1924, Ransome and Evgenia were married in Riga and, keen to settle down, returned to Lakeland. Evgenia was described to me as a huge, unique and generous person. Strong and formidable, topped by a mass of black hair, she had a booming voice that tended to stay on the same note. At times, even Arthur must have found her awesome. There was a practical side to Evgenia. Indoors, she was a splendid cook, fussy about Arthur's diet. He must have nothing cooked in aluminium. Evgenia became noted for her excellent fish pies. Her favourite pets were cats.

At Low Ludderburn, Arthur regained something of his boyhood enthusiasm for Lakeland. I would have been delighted, as Editor of *Cumbria*, to interview him but was told that his wife was sternly protective. (Rupert Hart-Davis referred to her as "the boss"). I was advised to keep away from their secluded Lakeland home. Ransome did feature in the magazine via articles and letters-to-the-editor. Most of my information about her was by word of mouth. I was told that Evgenia had cleared stones from the side of the hill to create a garden. The drystone wall she constructed with her bare hands was durable, though local people, especially farmers, had forecast it would soon fall down.

At Nibthwaite, I spent a pleasant afternoon with Brigit, youngest child of the Altounyan family who was to become a founder of the Arthur Ransome Society. Her face was wizened but there was brightness in her eyes and speech. (Later in the Ransome story, as Bridget, she would have a part to play in the story entitled *Secret Water).* Arthur Lupton, Ransome's nephew – tall, brisk, purposeful and precise of speech – had retired to the Dales town of Settle. We often met. One day he related how there had been fatherly worries concerning Young Arthur. He was thought to be frittering his brains away, a process known as "Arthur's bright ideas". Arthur Lupton recalled Uncle Arthur as being big, very loud and bristly. He wore rough tweeds. "We were in awe of him."

The nephew had character. I watched enthralled as Arthur Lupton delivered a wordless rebuke to the driver of a car that, at a road junction, had crossed a white line for several feet on to the main road along which Arthur was cycling. When his stretch of tarmac was impinged on, Arthur braked, coming squeakily to a halt with one of his feet resting on a pedal and the other on the road. No word was spoken. The intruding motorist seemed to shrivel under a ten-second glare. Arthur then continued his cycle-run into town.

When I met Sir Rupert Hart-Davis at his retirement home in Marske, near Richmond, Yorkshire, the name of Arthur Ransome was bound to be mentioned. Hart-Davis (1907-1999) had been Ransome's friend and literary executor who, on the death of the author, had published autobiographical information. Hart-Davis, keen on sport, especially cricket and rugby, did not share Ransome's passion for angling and had little respect for Ransome's widow. She had made his relationship with Arthur difficult. (When Arthur was old and decrepit, Hart-Davis would drive him to his favourite angling haunts, parking as close to water as possible).

Hart-Davis, as one of two literary executors, had overseen the publication of the Ransome autobiography following the death of Arthur and his wife. This so-called venomous woman would donate to the Museum of Lakeland Life and Industry, at Kendal, many personal objects. They included Ransome's desk, chair, lamp and the nucleus of his library, with first editions of his publications. Surprisingly, there was also a gift of a carved raven in wood, of Russian origin, an object that had inspired Ransome when writing. Today it is "perched" on his

Arthur Ransome's second wife Evgenia. Cats were her favourite pets. (Brotherton Library, University of Leeds)

desk along with his pipes, tobacco tin and a small compass.

I felt close to Arthur Ransome when visiting the Special Collections section of the Brotherton Library of Leeds University, the recipient of a large quantity of Ransome material. Arrayed before me were such personal items as a diary, a working notebook and a variety of photographs, one featuring his favourite cats, Polly and Podge, offspring of a cat known as Sally. They had been photographed at Low Ludderburn, in the Winster Valley, a retreat in every sense. As noted, it was in the converted bank-barn of this former farmhouse that Ransome typed *Swallows and Amazons*.

Entries in his diaries dealt tersely, in diminutive writing, with events such as birds seen in his garden and angling experiences he had been fond of recalling.

Living in style in a large house that stood on the other side of the Winster Valley was Colonel Kelsall. The two men, passionate about angling, evolved a complex visual signalling system which came into play when they had angling jaunts in mind, relating to conditions and prospects. There were some social connections. Arthur had tea at the Colonel's home and they had picnicked together.

Most of the Ransome letters preserved at Leeds University had been written to Edith, his mother, whom he adored. Now and again he would illustrate a few handwritten paragraphs with a human figure. Ransome typed almost everything else, as I saw when glancing at handwritten aspects of one of the books at which he had been working. A story headed *The River Comes First* was never published in its entirety.

Arthur Ransome with one of his favourite cats. (Brotherton Library, University of Leeds)

The hero of the tale was given the common name of Tom. Mention was made of the Bela, a fishable river that flows into Kent Estuary. We may never get to know what happened to Tom.

Ransome lived at an especially happy time for Lakeland authors. The area lived largely for itself. Local life had not yet been smothered by bureaucracy and mass tourism. Most of the residents were native-born. Almost every village supported a range of craftsmen, such as blacksmith and joiner.

As an emissary of *Cumbria*, I joyfully recorded the folk activity of "Ransome time", interviewing boatmen, farmers, wrestlers, hound-trailers and the charcoal-burners.

My quest to discover the origin of the boats in *Swallows and Amazons* led me to Crossfields' boatyard, between Arnside Knott and the Kent estuary. Here was fashioned *Swallow*, a sea-going sailing boat that features in Ransome's Lakeland yarns. Francis John Crossfield, who died in 1935 at the age of 85, may have been personally known to Ransome. Towards the end of the 19th century, and into the 20th, the Crossfield speciality was building fishing boats and cruising yachts. About 400 of their boats, their lengths ranging from 18 to 50 feet, took to the water.

Arthur Ransome wrote using a steel-nibbed pen or his faithful old typewriter, which was one of the early portable variety. Almost everything was typed. He usually had a pipe in his mouth, into the bowl of which had been packed Black Kendal Twist. It was Arthur's favourite brand of tobacco which – according to his friend Edward Thomas - was "strong enough to knock out the unaccustomed southerner like a blow from a battering ram." Through his books, Ransome made the Lakeland landscape live. He dealt with everyday life. He mixed up topography in his creation of Wild Cat Island, Houseboat Bay and the Amazon River. Coniston Old Man became Kanchenjunga, ruler of the High Topps. Bowness Bay, with its range of lofty wooden boat-sheds, was given the literary tag of Rio, presumably from Rio Grande. God-like, he positioned the North Pole not so far away.

Arthur had been educated at Old College, a prep school at Windermere. His academic advances and his relationship with other boys were stilted by short-sightedness, of which no one seemed aware. Among his vivid memories was the Great Frost of 1895, when Windermere – the lake, that is – froze from end to end. By good fortune, the headmaster of Old College was fond of skating. Such a freeze-up was rare; he would excuse his boys from lessons and encourage them to develop their ice-skating skills.

The frozen lake teemed with skaters by day and at night they operated by lantern-light. Carriages were driven across the ice and ice-yachts were raced. (When the lake froze over in 1929, Ransome was to have some fresh experiences for his book *Winter Holiday*, published in 1933. Captain Flint's houseboat, iced-in and immovable, was compared with *Fram*, which was similarly immobilised – in the Antarctic!). Arthur entered the illustrious Rugby School without a scholarship; he had failed the crucial examination. He was hopeless at sport. Not being able to see the ball at cricket or football led to him being bullied. He began to wear spectacles.

Sporting aspects of the Old Lakeland had a strong

A remarkable scene from 1895, when Windermere froze from end to end.

appeal. When young, he tried his hand at Cumberland & Westmorland style wrestling – said to have been introduced by the Vikings – and he was also captivated by hound-trailing, the trail being laid by dragging some flavoured rag around a stretch of fell-country. In due course, he would be taught sailing by new-found friends, the Collingwoods, whose home overlooked the top end of Coniston Water. Sailing-dinghies were to become major props in his children's adventure stories.

Throughout his life, Ransome was haunted by conflicting memories of his father, who had died in 1897, aged 46. Medically, father had gone downhill after he tumbled over an old grindstone while returning from an angling jaunt by Coniston Water. What was assessed as a sprained ankle became tubercular, leading to the affected leg being amputated to the knee, then to his thigh. (He had resigned from his academic connection with Leeds and moved the family to Rugby).

As for Arthur, books were a prime interest. Impulsively, after a spell at Yorkshire College, he abandoned a chemistry degree to become an errand boy, a menial job, for a London publisher. He had a foot on the bottom rung of the literary ladder.

Destination Lakeland

I am ahead of myself. Cyril and Edith Ransome, the parents of Arthur, were married at Wem Church, in Shropshire, and had four children. Arthur Mitchell was born on January 18, 1884, the others being Joyce, Geoffrey and Cecily. (Mitchell, the surname of his godfather, was dropped from Arthur's name at an early date). The family home, 6 Ash Grove, Headingley, was a detached villa-like house tucked away in a less busy part of the city. It is now usually lined with parked cars, though trees shade some of the gardens and there is even a springtime patch of daffodils.

Cyril had a respected academic status, being Professor of History at Yorkshire College,

Old farm buildings at Nibthwaite.

Opposite: Old Hall Farm, a characteristic Lakeland dwelling at Nibthwaite. Young Arthur was "free in paradise" in this locality.

subsequently the University of Leeds. He earned extra cash by writing history books for schools. Edith, a woman with a strong personality, had a special interest in watercolour painting.

In Victorian Leeds, the clip-clop of horses' hooves on a hard road was a dominant sound, as Cyril recorded in his diary for 1884 when the clip-clopping was between the house and railway station. "This year," he noted, "we began to go to Mr John Swainson's, Nibthwaite, a farmhouse at the foot of Coniston where we have spent some of our happiest hours and the children enjoyed a full taste of country life." Cyril's passion being for angling, the highpoint of his year was that long summer term spent by Coniston Water.

A city lad, Arthur would enjoy the rail journey from Leeds to Greenodd, where the Swainsons would provide horse-drawn transport to their destination. From Leeds, the train clattered through the Aire Gap, with the wheels beating a tattoo - *de de de deh* – on jointed rails. Arthur, glancing towards the Pennines, would, around Long Preston, see millstone grit give way to the pearl-grey ramparts of the most extensive limestone outcrop in the land. As the train accessed the Lune Valley from Clapham, a tree-lined River Wenning was in view. At Carnforth they switched to the Furness route. The train clattered on a viaduct spanning the Kent Estuary.

Arthur was to recall their journey on the coastal line as "a good old, stinking, third-class Furness railway carriage with lots of miners going up Millom way." The railway, which "we always counted as peculiarly our own", ran on an embankment that provided the little town of Grange-over-Sands with a breakwater. In pre-railway days the tide had an annoying habit of advancing as far as the main street. Across a low-tide bay, men with horse-drawn carts were trawling tide-washed gutters on Morecambe Bay for shrimps and a flatfish called fluke.

The family disembarked at Greenodd, a once busy little port where the River Crake ran into the estuary of the Leven. A Directory of 1851 associated the place with "a steam saw mill, a ship building and hoop-monger's establishment, besides a tan yard, coal yards and several other trades..." Up to thirty horses with wagons were used to transport timber from local estates. A special siding was available for the reception of gunpowder from Black Beck, at Bouth.

The four-mile journey to Nibthwaite was by horse-drawn vehicles. In clear weather, the Ransomes would see a western skyline crowned by Coniston Old Man. Cyril, in love with angling, would call a halt at Lowick Bridge so he might scan the water. And in next-to-no-time after arriving at Nibthwaite, he would go off fishing, though not before consuming the afternoon tea prepared by Mrs Swainson.

Young Arthur was "free in paradise", kneeling at an old stone quay so he might dip his hand in the lake – proof that he had come home. At that time, the lake supported shoals of minnows. He caught some in the cutting where the Swainsons moored their boat. A group of stones was dubbed *Gondola*, after the lake steamer. He slid down a rock he called the Knickerbockerbreaker because of the wear-and-tear on that item of clothing. When threadbare, these trousers were darned *in situ* by Annie

Swainson.

Arthur's autobiography, published in 1976, revealed sights and sounds of that half-forgotten time.

At Swainson's farm he had to ensure that the butter-churn was in its proper place. In the kitchen, a grandfather clock was "whirring wheezily" as it struck the hours. There was no indoor flush-toilet. An earth closet, "with its three sociable seats", was to be found in the garden, with two seats for adults; a small middle one accommodated a baby. (The walls of the closet were papered with pages from the magazine *Punch).* Young Arthur ventured into the cowsheds. He kept clear of a muckheap in the farmyard. Apart from the smell, it was not as substantial as it looked, as he discovered when leaping on to it from an orchard wall. The Swainsons' haycart was painted blue and red. Damson trees adorned the orchard.

I set foot in Nibthwaite in 1984, after circling the lake on narrow roads. A view of Peel Island evoked memories of Ransome's books. As a young man, he had camped there on several occasions and so did young folk in *Swallows and Amazons.* (My son and his family, staying on a caravan site at Coniston, twice rowed a boat to Peel and had Ransome's best-known book in mind as they explored the island).

A glimpse of Brantwood, on the eastern side of Coniston Water, reminded me that this was the residence of John Ruskin. Ransome, in his later years, occasionally glimpsed the secretive old man.

At Kirkby-in-Furness, I met a man aged 106 who had special memories of Ruskin. He related how, as a boy, he was visiting an aunt at Coniston, when –

unexpectedly – into the house came an old man with a long grey beard. John Ruskin was escaping from his domineering relatives, who soon arrived to collect him. Ruskin used the home of the Coniston lady as a sanctuary because she had worked at Brantwood and, unlike his relatives, treated him kindly.

On my motor run round Coniston Water, I glimpsed Lanehead, the former, mansion-like home of the Collingwood family with which Ransome would become closely connected. In Coniston village, I stood before the ornate cross, designed by W G Collingwood, and marking Ruskin's last resting place. (Collingwood was interred not far away). Then I drove west of the Water and back to Nibthwaite with a recollection of fells sharply delineated in the still waters. Cormorants, mallard, pochard and even the odd merganser left silver wakes on this day of unbroken sunshine.

Happily, Nibthwaite is still much as Arthur must have known it. A little bridge crosses the beck. The Victorian letterbox is still set in a drystone wall at the bend of the road. Old-time recesses where bee-skeps were kept have not been filled in. Quite by chance, I was introduced to Brigit Sanders, who had personal memories of Ransome and his most celebrated book.

Much of Cyril Ransome's three-month break from academic life had been spent angling. Cyril loved his son Arthur but, unhappily, was poor at dealing with him. They had a mutual good feeling for the hills and lakes of the Furness area and particularly the finny inhabitants of the lakes. Arthur was to write that "those holidays at Nibthwaite I owe to my father's passion for the lake country. They bred a similar passion in me that has lasted my life and

Brantwood, home of John Ruskin, on the eastern side of Coniston Water.

Steam power at Haverthwaite station on the line to Lakeside. The lower part of this line was familiar to the Ransome family, who would join the train at Greenodd in order to return to Leeds.

been the mainspring of the books I have been happiest in writing."

Some local features were re-named. Alan Tarn, on the River Crake, not far from Nibthwaite, was an expanse of water, rich in water-lilies. To Arthur, it assumed the menacing name of Octopus Lagoon. Meanwhile, his mother would be sketching, using watercolours, and father bestrode the lake shores, looking for suitable places to "cast his flies."

Migratory fish – salmon and sea trout – ran upriver in numbers. So common were they it was possible to lift them from the water. (Alas, in the not-too-distant future, disease would lead to a decline in the salmon stock).

As a salmon river, the Leven, with its greater flow of water, was supreme. Arthur would have the joy of landing a seven-pound salmon. While father fished, or shot grouse on the hills, and while mother sketched, Young Arthur was fascinated by what he was to describe in his autobiography as "the seething squirming mass of eels". Many eels, bound for the Sargasso Sea, were captured in an eel-coop by the mill. Eels, migrating on dark nights, were diverted into the mill-race, part of which was, in effect, a wooden box with laths to release the water but hold the eels, which at the time I visited it were being sold in a Manchester market.

Lakeland was industrialised. Labour was cheap. An eleven-year-old lad who started work at the Coniston copper mines was paid 4s a week, compared with the guinea paid to an adult. Quarrymen became miners as they hollowed out noble crags for the best slate. In the extensive coppice woods, Arthur was to meet the so-called charcoal-burners. They spent their summers in wigwam-type structures handy to their pitsteads, from which rose plumes of blue-grey smoke. The makers of swills [plaited wooden baskets] wove their products from coppice oak boiled and riven into strips.

In lean times, folk went into a state of semi-hibernation. During the Great Slump of the 1920s and 30s, top men on the farms were lucky if they earned £1 a week. Lads were "gitting about four or five pund for t'alf year." They were expected to work seven days a week. The effect on stock prices was alarming, with the very best of sheep bringing "six bob a head." The inter-war depression was acute in 1932, a time when Ransome was busily writing his *Swallows* series of children's adventure stories.

An entertaining story told by Young Arthur and re-told for my benefit by Arthur Lupton, his nephew, concerned the end of yet another invigorating summer holiday – an end that was tinged with melancholy as the family prepared to leave Greenodd for Leeds. As the Ransomes crossed the line to reach the appropriate platform, the train from Lakeside came into view. Arthur was carrying a large cardboard box, the interior divided by partitions and smaller boxes. These held his holiday collection of "livestock" – caterpillars, newts, lizards – along with pieces of their natural food. With the train bearing down on him, he slipped, the box opened and the contents were scattered on the track which would be used by the approaching train. The stationmaster came to his aid by reversing the signals, holding up the train at a distance of a few yards. He then helped Young Arthur to rescue his menagerie.

Wild Cat Island

On an autumn day at the lower end of Coniston Water, I had a bad attack of Ransomitis, a yearning to clamber into a rowing-boat heading for Peel Island, a minor feature – small, rocky, tufty with trees – in the grand Lakeland scene. It is best seen from near Nibthwaite, where its small size and tuftiness are clear to see. View it from the west shore of Coniston Water and it is apt to blend with the woodland east of the lake. Formerly known as Montagu Island, and now owned by the National Trust, this small island with a big history was visited by the Ransomes during their summer vacations. If father remained in the boat, fly-fishing for trout, mother, a keen watercolourist, might settle down with paper, brush and paint. Arthur recalled that "we children spent the day as savages". Back at the farm, trout caught by father, as he drifted by the shore of the lake, were cooked by Mrs Swainson for tomorrow's breakfast.

Arthur wrote about the islet in his book *Pond and Stream.* The Collingwood girls had visited the place and recalled*:* "We row down the lake, lazily and slowly... A little more than half way down there is an island that we can see, a green dot in the distance, from our farmhouse windows, and here we have our tea... We prowl over the rockiness of the little island, and creep among the hazels and pines and tiny oaks and undergrowth..." In *Swallows and Amazons,* Peel Island was glamorised as Wild Cat Island. My old friend A H Griffin, a native of Furness, described the island as "a wooded knuckle of rock raised above the lower reaches of Coniston Water. It is a lovely place, carpeted in summer with bluebells, heather and ferns..."

During the inter-war years, the Ransomes swam, rowed, fished and also camped on Peel Island, though it is neither large nor sufficiently varied to have been a sole inspiration for the fictional Wild Cat Island. Perhaps, in Ransome's literary mind, it was amalgamated with Blakeholme on Windermere. The Wild Cat Island of Ransome's imagination had a secluded harbour, a camp site and a lofty pine that became known as Lighthouse Tree when a lantern was raised.

My urge to explore the island came with a glimpse of a drawing by Clifford Webb in the first edition of *Swallows and Amazons.* The artist, using strong lines, pictured a secluded cove, framed by large trees, with upsweeping rock in the background. A sailing dinghy, drawn up on the beach, was being attended by three children – from the quartet known as Swallows. Ransome had been captivated by rocks that flanked a natural harbour. As the island was approached, Captain John unshipped the rudder and laid it at the bottom of the boat, skulling over the stern, providing just enough power to ensure that *Swallow* would move gradually towards the lines of rocks.

I had read Collingwood's impressions, as recorded in a new edition of *The Lake Counties*, which had been revised by the author in 1932 and reprinted with revisions in the following year. The author

The anchorage, Peel Island, which was
often visited by the Ransomes during their
summer holidays.

referred his readers to Mr Arthur Ransome's recent books, these being *Swallows and Amazons* and *Swallowdale.* They would doubtless recognise the place, "altered a little by the usual literary camouflage, but with all its charms preserved."

Collingwood observed that with a near view of Peel Island the resemblance of a ship of old times was increased by a diminutive "calf rock". This was like "a boat in tow at its stern, joined to the main rock at low water by a narrow ridge, beside which there is a pretty little cove for harbour and a well-blackened fire-spot where many a picnic kettle has boiled." Collingwood, digging hereabouts, had found medieval pottery and an old smithy-hearth. "In May the island is a mass of bluebells; later in the summer, bell-heather and fern blend their colours; in autumn the varied foliage is singularly rich against the background of distant blue."

Rowing near Peel Island – a "gladsome experience."

It was on Peel Island, in 1895, when Arthur was eleven years of age, that the Ransome family met the Collingwoods and shared a picnic. It was a chance encounter that would have a lasting effect. On a future occasion, Arthur – now a friend of the family and staying with them – revisited Peel Island in the company of the Collingwood children – Robin, Barbara, Dora and Ursula. The picnic fare was "a bun-loaf, a pot of marmalade and a kettle." Arthur camped on the island in 1910. He was completing his book on Edgar Allan Poe and it is related that Ursula transported the proofs to him in a novel way – tied on the top of her head. When the proofs had been corrected, they were transported to the shore in a similar fashion – and in time to catch the post!

Nearly eighty years have elapsed since, in the famous tale, John, Susan, Titty and Roger Walker sailed in the *Swallow* to camp on Wildcat Island, where they were challenged by Nancy and Peggy Blackett, who were operating under the name of Amazons. They knew the island well and, at first, they resented it being taken over by the Swallows. A friendship between the two crews was established. Both now turned on the Blacketts' uncle, nicknamed Captain Flint, whose temporary home was a houseboat. He wanted some peace while he wrote a book. He was classified as a pirate!

The film version of *Swallows and Amazons*, set in 1929, gloriously recaptured the spirit of the book, both pictorially and musically. Such action and scenes must have flashed through the mind of Arthur Ransome as he composed it on a clattering typewriter in the converted bank-barn in a setting of thick woodland, to the east of Windermere town. The film begins with a train trip on the Lakeside line, then switches to Coniston Water, with the children running excitedly down a sloping field for a glimpse of Peel Island. Father's permission for the voyage had been requested. He was serving in the Navy, based in Malta. His agreement, recorded in the book, then vividly in the film, is unforgettable: "Better drowned than duffers; if not duffers, won't drown." In the film, Roger asks: "Does that mean yes?" Mother thought so.

The uncle who features strongly in the latter part of the story is made to walk the plank. As his eyes were being bandaged, he hoped they were using a clean handkerchief. In the cabin was a squawky green parrot – a "pirate's parrot" for it was capable of saying "Pieces of Eight." At the end of the film, the camera focuses on some of the goodies – a quivering jelly and a cake adorned by representations of the two boats – *Swallow* and *Amazon* – sailing on a lake of blue-tinted icing. The holiday was pronounced "grand". Titty hoped that such holidays would take place "next year and for all the other years, for ever and ever…"

Not long before I had the gladsome experience of being rowed out to Peel Island, I visited the Steamboat Museum at Bowness and, with the owner's permission, boarded *Esperance*, the craft which, with some modifications, had been used as the houseboat in a cinema version of *Swallows and Amazons*. A parrot – one of the soft-toy variety – had been placed beside a window in the cabin in memory of Captain Flint. My excursion to Wild Cat Island began when a friend who owned a rowing-boat that was laid up on the wooded south-western shore of the lake offered to row me there. Having misplaced the boat's plug, he filled the hole with a twig. Hopefully, it would swell in contact with water. This novel gesture would surely have appealed to Ransome. (The missing plug was eventually found in the dashboard locker of the owner's car).

The rowing-boat was launched onto a lake that was being strummed by a light northerly wind, which "cleared the air". The hills flanking Coniston Water now had the clarity of a fine etching. An aerial escort was provided by two mute swans. In a district wearing a Joseph's Coat of Many Colours, the only eyesore was a cluster of wind-turbines that were peeping over Broughton Moor. I concentrated on sensations near at hand, such as the distinctive sound of wavelets lapping against the bows of the boat. Such sounds had a strong appeal for Arthur Ransome. Scanning the western skyline, I picked out the Coniston Old Man, which to him, in another of his books, was dubbed Kilimanjaro. One of Ransome's cherished possessions was a lucky stone – a stone with a hole through it – picked up on Coniston Old Man. Having climbed the Old Man once or twice, and now looking at the great fell from the vantage point of a boat, I fancied that the fell winked back at me.

My new friend rowed the boat with experienced ease. *Swallow,* as recorded by Ransome, had flaunted a large brown sail. A plume of white smoke in the distance emanated from the steamboat *Gondola.* Into my mind flashed a picture of the grand old vessel during the time it was beached and ignored near Nibthwaite. A joyful experience during my editorship of *Cumbria* magazine followed its rescue and restoration by the National Trust. On re-launch day, I was provided with a dinghy so I might view the proceedings from the lake. The restored boat entered the water stern-first.

Now, at the approach to Peel Island, my friend deftly positioned his rowing-boat between natural jetties formed of lines of wave-smoothed rock. With the dinghy tethered to a tree, we explored the island, following well-used tracks. In addition to conifers I recognised some of the indigenous tree species: oak, hazel and holly. Blackberries were there to be picked. Ling and bell heather grew rank because there were no browsing sheep to trim them. The northern end was not a place in which to linger. It lay in shadow, strummed by a strengthening wind. The central valley – as a shallow depression might be called – evoked memories of W G Collingwood, who carried out excavations and, reckoning that Norse settlers had fortified the place, was inspired by Peel Island to write a saga he entitled *Thorstein of the Mere.* The book, published in 1895, was an inspiration to Young Arthur Ransome.

Collingwood wrote: "In the midst of Thurstan-water there is a little island, lying all alone. When you see it from the fells, it looks like a ship in the blue ripples; but a ship at anchor while the mere moves upbank or downbank, as the wind may be. The little island is ship-like also because its shape is long and its sides are steep with no flat and shelving shores; but a high short nab there is to the northward for a prow, so to speak; and a high sharpness to the southward, for a poop. And to make the likeness better still, a long narrow calf-like rock lies in the water, as if it were the cockboat at the stern; while tall trees stand for masts and sails."

Thorstein's first impressions of the lake are fresh and lively. After slogging northwards, by a waterway and through woodland, his heart beat hard when the wood thinned, the waterway broadened, the world grew brighter "and, lo, beyond, a great gleam of blue and a blaze of golden sky." He climbed a howe (hill) on the left. As he climbed, the lake opened up before him.

"Beyond the nearer woods there was the deep of blue and the lonely island in the midst of it; and from his feet, away into the uttermost distance, the huge fells, tossing like the breakers on a stormy beach and rolling away and afar like the heaving waves of the sea."

Thorstein ran down to the shore. He stripped off hood and kirtle, hose and shoes, all stained and ragged with scrambling through break and briar. Wading into deep water, he plunged "and swam

Gondola, emitting its familiar plume of
white smoke.

The rowing boat deftly positioned on Peel Island between natural jetties of wave-smoothed rock.

steadily through the calmness." Creeping ashore, he donned his clothes, then "looked about him for a safe night-lair…" Was Peel Island named after ancient fortifications, traces of which were found? The plant life is profuse and varied. My sailing friend and I found a sheltered spot on sun-warmed rocks to the south of the island and here had our snack meal, looking at the local features: the hills, the woods and a row of wind turbines somewhere over by Broughton Moor. Happily they were dwarfed by distance.

The Swallows, on a camping trip, were well-equipped and provisioned. My friend and I sat on the rocks, munching sandwiches and washing them down with tea from thermos flasks. Our talk was mainly about Ransome. He had associated Peel Island with Wild Cats and later used *Wild Cat* for the name of a schooner in his book *Peter Duck*. Collingwood had compared the island with a ship at anchor, adding: "The little island is ship-like also because its shape is long and its sides are steep." It had a high, short nab to the northward for a prow and a high sharp ness to the southward for poop. The "long narrow calf rock" that Collingwood compared with a cockboat at the stern of a ship was the spot from which I would clamber into the dinghy for the return to the mainland.

On Wild Cat Island I pondered on Arthur Ransome's associations with the Lake District. He lived at a time when three counties – Cumberland, Westmorland and Lancashire (North of the Sands) – had wedge-shaped slices of what is now referred to blandly as Cumbria. Winter darkness was relieved not by electrical glare but by the cold light of a full moon and by pin-pricks of light from paraffin lamps at cottages and farms. The tourist season began at Easter and ended in October. Few people walked for pleasure. The grizzle-grey farmers had little time for anything else but their sheep. Farming was a way of life, not an industry. Villagers made their own fun. I had an old Ford car which – on a soggy day in Borrowdale – gave me a sinking feeling. Composite boarding, which someone had fitted to the floor, had lost its rigidity. Happily, I was not far from a joiner. At Keswick, I stood by as he fitted some wooden floorboards. And creosoted them!

A tip about the origins of the celebrated dinghy known as *Swallow* prompted me to visit Fred Crossfield's boathouse at Arnside. This small but notable enterprise occupied a cleft of limestone and was overhung by enormous beech trees. Three generations of boat-building Crossfields had transformed oak and larch into seaworthy Morecambe trawlers and other craft, such as *Swallow*, which was to spend its busy life on freshwater. The firm closed down with the retirement of Fred Crossfield in 1950.

Meet the Collingwoods

On a day that was mild enough to warm the slaty joints of Coniston Old Man, a virtually naked Ransome, with romantic poetry in mind, sprawled on a rock beside the gushing water of Coppermines Beck. That day, his life was changed through an encounter with W G Collingwood, a distinguished local resident who had climbed the Old Man on a painting jaunt. Collingwood was startled on his descent to see what he at first took to be a naked corpse. The corpse stirred. Arthur Ransome revealed himself. The two men chatted.

Collingwood took the young man home and introduced him to his family – to his wife, son and three daughters. It was a tremendous boost to Ransome. An adult was taking him seriously! Collingwood, on becoming John Ruskin's amanuensis and friend, had moved from a cottage near Gillhead, by Windermere, to Lanehead, an imposing house situated beside the woods of Monk Coniston. Lanehead evolved from a wayside inn, on the site of which a member of the Braythwaite family built what might be classified as "a gentleman's residence." The owner of nearby Tent Lodge made it available to Collingwood, writer, artist and, notably, secretary to John Ruskin of Brantwood.

Ransome was absorbed into the Collingwood family circle from 1904 onwards, which meant he might regard Lanehead as a home. He never forgot his first visit. His lower jaw must have dropped with astonishment as he entered Collingwood's sanctum – the study of a scholar – to see a long table obscured by manuscripts and books stacked from floor to ceiling. An unfinished painting reposed on an easel. Writing materials were displayed on a small table.

Collingwood brought happiness and a sense of purpose into the life of Ransome, who had been a bemused young man. It was through the Collingwood connection that he learned to sail. Ransome's storytelling was in part inspired by reading Collingwood's book *Thorstein of the Mere*, which had a Norse theme. Not everyone liked Collingwood's imaginative tales. His Norse stories, in particular, tended to be heavy-going. Yet it was this gentle scholar who encouraged Ransome in his writing and, equally important, he offered him tuition in the rudiments of sailing.

Collingwood's skill as a writer was in straightforward historical analysis and research. This is evident in an extract plucked from his book *The Lake Counties* (1902): "Coniston Water is a singular instance of nature's *vis medicatrix,* the way she heals old sores. Along the beach in every little dell where an unfailing streamlet runs down, there used to be iron furnaces [bloomeries], where small charges of ore, brought on pack-horses and boats from Low Furness, were smelted with charcoal. The woods had been almost destroyed.

"We can imagine a period when the barren hills were only varied by smoking 'pitsteads', where charcoal was made, and flaming 'hearths' where grimy workers toiled at the bellows, or shovelled the red ore and black coals, with shouts and rattling, and

Coniston railway station, photographed shortly after closure, which in its heyday brought in thousands of visitors to the area.

the thud of the little waterwheels that worked the hammers and drove the blast. Perhaps not all the scene was at any one time so filled, but that was the character of the place."

And now, he added, "there is no such dainty frondage and foliage, no such utter peace and stillness, as in the caves and crannies of the water's edge, where softly rowing you may start the otter and the kingfisher, and hear no more but the splash of the leaping trout, and the distinguishable call of many streams – this one tinkling, that one gurgling, and one beyond belling through the woods, and another across a mile of water chattering over the stones or roaring down the coppice-hidden ravine." When *The Lake Counties* was re-published in 1931, Sir Hugh Walpole wrote in *The Times:* "A friend of mine has described it as 'the finest guide book in English'; but it is, of course, far more than a guide-book, for it contains the grandest prose-writing about the Lake District in existence..."

Ransome was to describe in his autobiography his first meeting with the talented Lanehead family. Mrs Collingwood and the girls both fascinated and terrified the sensitive young man. He had encountered a polymath circle of a type that he would not often encounter in later life. The Collingwoods were talented in so many ways. Sailing had been elevated to a passion.

WG Collingwood became acquainted with Ruskin at Oxford during studies in philosophy and aesthetics. Collingwood married Edith Isaac, the daughter of an Essex corn merchant, and they settled in Lakeland. After Ruskin's death, in 1897, Collingwood planned a memorial exhibition at Coniston. He followed it with an idea for a Ruskin Museum in the village. Then came a trip to Iceland.

Ransome with his only child Tabitha. born in May 1910.

Bill Rollinson, a Lakeland historian, drew my attention to this rather special Icelandic link. During a hectic pony tour in 1897, Collingwood had recorded, in Indian ink or paint, the life of Icelanders on the sagasteads. His pictures formed a unique record of the period. Visiting Iceland in 1988, I joyfully discovered that his work was the subject of a special exhibition at the National Museum. As a student of the Icelandic language, he detected affinities between the speech, placenames and dialect of the Lake District.

The Coniston of W G Collingwood was that of twenty years on either side of the turn of the century. Coniston – or Cunniston, as the native calls it – had during the 19th century been like a frontier boom town, mainly through the tremendous development of the mines. By the time Collingwood was active, the copper mines had passed their heyday and were in almost terminal decline. There were still many quarrymen.

It was also, by Collingwood's time, becoming an important tourist centre. The railway was bringing 1,000 people at a time on outings. By the 1890s, Coniston was geared up in a big way to cater for tourists. And due in no small measure to Collingwood's influence, the village had become in the early part of the century the artistic centre of the Lake District.

When Arthur Ransome became a member of this influential family circle, it included three attractive daughters. Ransome was to write: "It would have been a monstrous freak of nature if I had not fallen in love with one or other of those girls." He fancied marrying Barbara, but she "had the good sense not to fall in love with me." He proposed to Dora. His proposal was not accepted but they continued to be friends.

Dora married Ernest Altounyan, whose father had founded a scientifically-based hospital at Aleppo in northern Syria. He qualified in medicine in England, then, having married Dora, returned to Syria. Their five children - Taqui, Susan, Mavis (invariably known as Titty), Roger and Brigit – returning to Lanehead for a summer holiday in 1928, would feature prominently in *Swallows and Amazons.*. That year, Ransome became "Uncle Arthur" to the Altounyans and, in the words of Brigit, when I met her at Nibthwaite, "he became interested in us, quite apart from his former friendship with my mother." Ransome was impressed by their exciting adventures. Back in London, he had found lodgings in the artist's quarter of Chelsea. With itchy fingers he penned his first book, *Bohemia in London.* It was a struggle to establish himself as a writer.

Ransome, keen to get married, successfully proposed to Ivy Constance Walker, whom he had met in London. She was an attractive young lady, two years his senior. Arthur was infatuated rather than in love with her, as he had been with Barbara. The infatuation was short-lived. Ivy's family, who were descended from landed gentry, objected to the match. Ivy was, after all, the daughter of a well-to-do solicitor.

Ransome, whose hope was to marry an ordinary young lady, became legally attached to one who was revealed to be somewhat snobbish, with a fondness for showing-off. They were married by special licence at a registry office in 1909. A church service followed. Ivy's family attended but were still rankled by the match. Fifteen months after the marriage, Ivy bore Arthur a daughter, who was christened Tabitha.

What did Ransome think of his marriage to Ivy? As usual, he confided in the written word, which is now tucked away in his collection of documents in the Brotherton Library. He thought Ivy would have been better and happier if she had married an actor or politician, someone who like herself was an extrovert. He blamed himself for the unhappy marriage; he had lacked the courage to run away before it was solemnised. He had been light-minded and idiotic in proposing to every young woman who had taken his fancy. Ivy was attractive to every young man who cast eyes on her. They were envious when Ransome married her.

During that unhappy marriage, his mind frequently strayed to the Lake District. On an autumnal visit, he pitched a lightweight tent for a night in the garden at Lanehead. He also camped on Peel Island. During a rare interlude – it was peaceful! – Arthur and Ivy lived in an old farmhouse in Wiltshire.

He had other things on his mind than marriage and fatherhood. He was a nomad by inclination. And he had a passion for the written word. In May 1913, Ransome, keen to make a break from Ivy, and having read a volume of Russian folk tales that had taken his fancy, fled to that country to collect and translate folk tales for a book on the title page of which his name would appear. He went back and forth to Russia, completing a folk tale mission. When *Old Peter's Russian Tales* was published in 1916 there were complimentary reviews in the press.

His storytelling phase ended abruptly in political turmoil. Ransome was persuaded to switch from folk-tale collector to journalist. He nonetheless kept in touch with his daughter through letters. Russia's torment was Revolution. From 1916 to 1919 he was the Russian correspondent of the *Daily News.* He then switched to the *Manchester Guardian*. He got to know Lenin and Trotsky, who – being notable Bolsheviks – were keen to make their views known to the British press. When Ransome's first-hand accounts of the troubles were published he came under the scrutiny of the British Secret Service.

Amid all this upheaval in Russian affairs, Ransome was introduced to Evgenia Shelepina, a tall, exuberant young lady who had been Trotsky's secretary. They were married. She would become Ransome's companion for the rest of his life. Now he yearned for a quiet time in his beloved Lake District. He wanted a measured life in which he might combine writing with pipe-smoking, angling and sailing. And so it was. In the Maytime of 1925, he and Evgenia settled in an obscure two-up, two-down home at Low Ludderburn, with a broad view of the quiet Winster valley.

Evgenia set about converting a venerable barn into a workroom. It was here that he would tap out on his venerable typewriter the draft of *Swallows and Amazons*. (The death of Ivy, his first wife, occurred in 1939. His attitude towards her had softened in later years). The children of *Swallows and Amazons* – who like Peter Pan never grew up – featured in four more novels with Lakeland settings, after which Ransome, his boat and typewriter switched to the Norfolk Broads and other southerly haunts.

Evgenia, the second wife of Arthur Ransome, had previously been Trotsky's secretary.
(Brotherton Library, University of Leeds)

Woodland Ways

For much of Arthur Ransome's life in Lakeland, the view from the window of his home took in the spectacle of massed trees. He was to write about a steep tract of land which, nonetheless, had been colonised by trees. He marvelled that little trees were able to cling on among the rocks. "There were all sorts of trees. Here and there was a tall pine, but most of the trees were oaks and beeches and hazels and mountain ash." In his day, coppice woods – this subtle harmony of young trees of native species - were a prominent feature of the landscape around Coniston Water and in some of the quiet little valleys.

Coppice woods were more valuable to a landowner than agricultural land. Every effort was made to keep farm stock out of the woods, and some tenant farmers were asked to leave if this rule went unheeded. Regeneration of coppice timber took place swiftly. Woodland where the dominant tree was hazel might be clear-felled again in twelve years or in about fifteen years in the case of oak woodland. Ransome watched groups of charcoal burners, commonly known as "coalers", at work.

He could tell such a worker by his dark complexion. And, spending so much time among smoke, his eyes looked watery.

Ransome introduced the crew of the *Swallow* to charcoal-burners – to Young Billie, aged over seventy, and his father, Old Billie, a still active ninety-four. They frequented woodland on the eastern shore of Coniston Water. The area was snake-infested. The two Billies showed their young visitors a fine specimen of an adder, our only poisonous snake, which they kept in a wooden box! Long years ago, an old lady caught three or four adders, having left a pan containing a little milk outside the house. The vipers located the milk and were drinking it. She simply put the lid on the pan – and placed it on the fire!

In *Swallowdale,* the charcoal-burners operated at Heald Wood, on the western side of the lake. Roger, having sprained an ankle, was given overnight accommodation in a cabin. In real life, a sturdy local man called George Davison lived comfortably in a succession of cabins at Stock Farm, Nibthwaite, into old age. George did not die in the cabin. "They got him to hospital. But he was proud and fond of his home."

Much woodland is now overrun with sheep; their browsing prevents natural regeneration and causes some trees to grow rough or "scroggy". Years ago, bountiful woodland yielded charcoal for gunpowder production, bark for tanning and young wood for a host of other profitable jobs. Winter was a time for felling trees, the season for "winter wood" ending on April 5. After that, only oak was cut, for the bark had to be acquired when the sap was running. Peeling of the bark was an occupation from May to the end of July, the bark being tied up and stored. Wet weather did not lead to idleness. The bark had to be chopped into two-inch lengths. In November, the men began to fell the next crop of trees.

The "coalers" of Furness were practising their arduous, uncomfortable but profitable craft well within the lifetime of Arthur Ransome. They were his neighbours. Some workers wore clogs. Woodmen preferred good, hand-sewn shoes. Charcoal-burning took place in what was known as a pitstead. The wood, stacked neatly, with a hole to admit fire, was covered with soil that had passed through a half-inch riddle. There followed a neat thatching of sods, slightly overlapping, to "turn bad weather."

In the 1970s, Jack Allonby, of Spark Bridge, was one of the few men who had personal recollections of "coaling". Jack re-created for his own interest, and the instruction of others, the type of living cabin used by the workers in Old Furness. Timbering was from coppice wood, secured with the use of axe and billhook. It was the type of cabin that four or five men might make during a working stint of several days at a time. Building a cabin could be done quickly. Said Jack: "All the materials were handy. When the men moved to another area, it was a simple job to make another cabin." With some patching up, it would last them for several years.

How was a cabin made? Picture a low circular wall with an inside diameter of twelve feet. The wall, made without a dab of mortar, is breached in two places – by a hearth and a doorway. Now picture a superstructure of timbering covered with sods and looking for all the world like a wigwam. Jack used a special long-shafted turf spade to obtain sods. He attempted to get them as thin as possible to minimise the weight. Covering an impressive eighty square yards took Jack two days. (This was a traditional living cabin. Who knows, it may have been the type of shelter made by the first men who settled in lowland Cumbria?).

Such a structure must be kept "aired". A fire that kept the men warm also kept at bay the fungi feeding on coppice wood. The hearth was substantial, a sheet of metal deflecting the flames and heat from the roof, which otherwise might easily catch fire. A cabin could be a smoky place. Building a chimney was a very particular job. If you didn't get it right, the fire would smoke badly. The chimney must be at the highest point or, said Jack, "t'draught would be t'wrong way." The door acts as the chimney, drawing the smoke. Sometimes rushes were spread on the floor of the cabin; otherwise the residents trod bare earth.

Their beds were simple structures. Four pronged sticks were driven into the ground and poles stretched between them. Birch chat [branches] was spread across the poles. A lucky coaler was given some straw by a local farmer. Straw was used to stuff the pillows! Workers in the coppice woods needed this durable accommodation. Quite often they had to walk over five miles from their homes to the work areas. Therefore it was best for them to lodge in the woods.

"Coalers" were fond of chewing tobacco or drawing the fumes of black twist up the stems of their briars. Arthur Ransome recorded that he was on speaking terms with charcoal-burners, some of whom baked clay pipes for him in the wood above Coniston. He collected them at the *Red Lion* at Lowick. The woodland workers entertained themselves with a variety of musical instruments – with fiddle, concertina, mouth organ or Jew's harp.

A charcoal burner's hut, constructed by Jack Allonby for the Hay Bridge Nature Reserve, Rusland Valley.

They dined mainly on ham, and bacon brought from home, for they were rarely lodging near a butcher's shop. Jack Allonby's father kept two pigs, especially for "coaling" time. The countryside might provide them with a few rabbits. Enough bread to last a week was kept in a large, mouse-proof tin. Rodents were attracted by the warmth of the cabin.

Burning began about the middle of August, with the season extending to the end of October, occasionally into November. Burners were paid an agreed sum per ton of charcoal. During the six weeks they lived in the woods, they neither washed nor shaved. Those who had cut the wood received money according to the number of bags in a pit, the average being about three and a-half dozen. If six dozen bags were used, the pit was reckoned to be a large one. At the pitstead, the charcoal-burners gave the heap of stacked wood a covering of rough water-grass, followed by soil, turf, more soil and more turf. All was then covered up so the wood would smoulder into charcoal and not burst into flame.

A "burn" began when a central pole was withdrawn and a ladle full of hot ashes was applied to the top of the heap. The fire worked its way out in a circle. If firing took place about 9-30 a.m, the "coalers" would begin "cooling" it at about two or three o'clock in the following afternoon. They were on duty overnight to ensure the fire remained covered. The workers were blackened by smoke and grime for, once started, the fire must not go out. The last "pit" was fired in 1924. This was six years before Ransome began his *Swallows* cycle of children's adventure tales. At that time, many a housewife ironed clothes using "charcoal irons". I chatted with a man whose mother had owned two such irons. The charcoal was put into the iron and kept glowingly hot by occasional bursts from a pair of bellows. With regard to "coaling", Jack Allonby told me: "Nobody's doing it now; it's all out-of-date."

A Visit to Rio

Arthur and Evgenia were fond of sailing on Windermere, the joy being intensified by afternoon tea ashore at Waterhead. When he wrote *Swallows and Amazons*, Windermere was handy for they were living at Low Ludderburn, just over the hill and the boat named *Swallow* had been moved from Coniston Walter to a boatyard at Bowness Bay. These surroundings were familiar. As you may recall, Arthur attended a prep school in Windermere – and ice-skated on the Bay during the Big Freeze of 1895.

Eighteen assorted islands lie like pieces of a jig-saw in the shallows between the two deep basins of Windermere. Belle Island, the largest, was notable for its large circular house and tidy grounds. Ransome probably had Silver Holme in mind for what he named Cormorant Island in the *Swallows and Amazons* series. (Holme is derived from the Old Norse). Ramp Holme and Blakeholme were islands on Windermere that, doubtless, contributed features to the romantic Wild Cat Island of his most famous book.

I had images of Ransome in mind whenever I sailed on Windermere. In 1976, I pictured him when travelling by launch towards Cockshott Point, heading for Bowness which Arthur, taking into account both lakeside and uphill sections, called Rio! A northerly wind did little more than ruffle the lake surface. Bowness Bay, the destination, was protected from the north wind and also from the prevailing south-wester. Elsewhere, it was not uncommon for a wind to be split by the flanking hills into several

distinct currents of air, so that gusts reach a boatman simultaneously from several directions.

Into my view, on that memorable sail, came Hartley Wife, the curious name for a rock. Who was Hartley? What happened to his wife? Did he leave her stranded on this smallest of islands where periodically the gulls alighted to rest and preen? Visitors hiring rowing boats at Bowness were tempted to land on the rock, despite the presence of warning buoys. A man standing on the rock shook his fist in mock anger as his companion rowed the boat away!

A rowing boat, Windermere style, had an average length of nineteen feet, was stylish, robust in appearance but clean in its lines, fashioned locally, mainly from locally-grown larch. Every plank had a distinctive shape. Larch, pitch pine or oak went to make the keel; the stem was of oak, naturally bent. Planks were positioned round wooden moulds that were later removed. The timbers were steamed into position and copper nails and brass screws were employed. When boats were first built at Bowness Bay, the copper nails were made by hand.

On my 1976 approach to Rio, I noticed that Curlew Crag, a name given to a few rocks ringed by buoys, was occupied by ducks. These were true Windermere ducks that had lost their fear of mankind. Some ducks have tolerated the near-presence of dogs. Massed in the shallows or along the beach, the ducks awaited visitors with paper bags which they knew from experience would contain

The magic of Bowness Bay on a summer evening.

scraps of food. Ducks waddled far from water. A pair nested on a boat, the owner of which – being well-disposed – would make the least possible use of the craft until the eggs hatched and the ducklings taken for their first swim.

All the places used by Arthur Ransome in his children's books were on the Ordnance Survey one-inch map, though – as he remarked to an inquirer – "the geography has been carefully confused." Much of the inspiration came from Windermere, long and narrow, roughly the same size and shape of Walney Island, off the Furness coast. Bowness, in its spacious bay, flanked by a row of boating huts, became the aforementioned Rio. Alas, the old-time boatyards that gave it a Rio-look were to be replaced by ultra-smart buildings. What Ransome referred to as the North Pole would disappear! Silver Holme was featured in *Swallows and Amazons* as Cormorant Island. Ransome arranged for the Amazon river to flow into the lake near Ambleside. Film-makers craved for Lakeland glamour. A version of *Swallows and Amazons* shot in the early 1980s appears to have Derwentwater as its setting!

In Ransome's time, the pace of life was slower, less garish. Ransome the Angler would almost certainly be familiar with char and also with char pie or potted char. He found pleasure in visiting Bowness, where anglers swapped stories of recent exploits on the lake and, traditionally, char was on sale at a butcher's shop. A local lady recalled gutting a fish, giving it a good wash, putting a knob of butter inside it, wrapping it in foil and slipping it into the oven. She said the flesh was more delicate than that of a trout.

For discerning anglers, eating a freshly caught char at the end of the day was a delectable experience. If anyone wanted more than a three-quarter pound char, served with all the trimmings, he would be a glutton. Char liked the cold depths except when spawning. During the summer of 1937 – Ransome time – a survey by the Freshwater Biological Association used an appliance with the ultra-scientific name of magneto-striction echo-sounding recorder. Three of the lakes dealt with – Windermere (north and south basins), Wastwater and Coniston Water – were found to have their deepest points below sea level.

Visiting Bowness Bay on a winter's day in 1954, I shared the shoreline with only three people – men with jobs to do. One was sweeping up the russet leaves of autumn and shovelling them into a wheelbarrow; another was tending a flower bed, and the third was cheerfully scrubbing some woodwork a few yards from the lake. A light mist had settled on the district. It was softly-toned, reflected by the calm lake, so that islands with their caps of trees seemed poised in the sky.

Four swans, one in the streaky plumage of youth, paddled gracefully by. The man scrubbing woodwork was Bert Hodgson, a boat proprietor. He was cleaning boats and oars with steel wool and soap before storing them away in his sheds for the winter. Bert had begun work in the local boat business when there was fierce competition, with many cut-price tactics employed to attract custom. In 1936, the boatmen banded themselves into an Association.

I visited a huddle of sheds along the fringe of the lake – the sheds Ransome had in mind when he dubbed the area Rio. Tom Storey, who had died in

Traditional Windermere rowing boats at Bowness Bay.

A largely traffic-free Bowness as it was in Ransome's time.

the previous year, was building boats at the age of ninety-six. At the workshops of Messrs Borwick, I met Bill Bland, a man who had begun boat-building in 1899. Bill, a native of Bowness, served his time with Tom Hayton, whose premises were demolished when the promenade was built just before the Great War. It was all handwork. Bill hand-sawed up to a dozen pairs of oars out of two and a-half inch planks at a time. Cutting out one pair of oars was an hour's work. Boats were of no fixed size and design. Craft up to fifty feet long were created in Tom Hayton's workshop. A first-class craftsman, apart from building boats he constructed the sheds that accommodated them.

Isaac Borwick was another name revered by Arthur Ransome. Isaac started a major firm in the early 1890s. In its robust history, boats of all kinds had their birth – yachts, motor launches, racing hydroplanes capable of high speeds and durable little rowing boats. The hydroplane type of craft was first built here in 1920. Like a giant wooden shoe, it was streamlined, adapted for skimming the water under power. There was one type of hydroplane which, at speed, touched the water in only two places, each merely the size of a hand.

Wilfred Shepherd, son of Nathaniel, who founded Shepherds, a major boat-builder, told me of the family's speciality, the Windermere-type of yacht, designed by P C Crossley and reportedly the fastest yacht in the world for its size. Yachting, said Wilfred, is like a game of billiards; "you never tire of it!" Alas, the glory days were past. Even in the 1950s, many enthusiasts for sailing were opting for mass-produced dinghies with sails. Yachts were being ruled out as a matter of expense.

In a roomy shed I saw nine yachts belonging to members of the Royal Windermere Yacht Club, which had its headquarters near the Old England Hotel. There were seventeen such yachts in existence. The weight of lead on the keel differed with each craft, one having 17 cwt and another perhaps 16 ½. The yachts also had slightly different overall weights. The governing factor was the length at the waterline, a matter of 17 feet.

The firm of Shepherds built the first motor boat in 1902. So unreliable was the first type of engine that Rio ached with cheers if an engine ran for half an hour without stopping. When a motor boat broke down, it had to be towed back to its moorings. As I wandered around a strangely deserted fringe of Bowness Bay, there were hammering sounds from the tall green sheds by the lake. In the gathering dusk I prepared to leave Bowness. Five people were in view, each of them hurrying as rain slanted down. I could not see a single boat on the lake. A flock of gulls squabbled for food. A swan arched its lovely neck to feed.

Swallows and Amazons

The children's adventure story named *Swallows and Amazons* – fresh and lively – caught for all time the spirit of a Lakeland waterborne holiday in the late 1920s. Margaret Drabble, in *A Writer's Britain* (1979), mentioned how Ransome and several other major authors had been influenced by the writings of Richard Jefferies, the Wiltshire author about rural life. His book *Bevis* became the prototype of a special type of imaginative adventure story set in the open air.

In a long appraisal of writing *Swallows and Amazons,* which forms part of an extensive archive at Leeds, Ransome wrote that the task had given him more pleasure than any of his other books. The pleasure was derived from his awareness that children do not distinguish between belief and reality. He had experienced this in childhood; it conceivably extended in adulthood. They were making the best of both worlds. He had enjoyed himself "like fun".

The story of the creation of *Swallows and Amazons,* which falls into the adventure story category, yet is distinctive in its treatment, began in the summer of 1928, when the Altounyans – Dora, her husband Ernest, and their five children – had a long summer holiday at Bank Ground Farm, close to grandparents' house at Lanehead. Arthur and Ernest bought two lug-sailed dinghies, which they named *Swallow* and *Mavis* and the children were taught how to use them. *Swallow* became the property of Arthur. *Mavis* was retained by Ernest.

The *Swallow*, a one-time fishing-boat, was described by Arthur as being "monstrously heavy to row but not bad under sail, the first of a long dynasty of *Swallows* in my sailing life." The holiday was packed with lakeborne adventures and when the Altounyans were about to return to their home in Syria, in January, 1929, the children gave Arthur an unusual birthday present – a pair of red, turned-up-at-the-toes Turkish slippers.

Another memory of those early days emerges from the dedication of the first edition of *Swallows and Amazons*: "To the six, in exchange for a pair of slippers." The slippers were the product of the Aleppo leather market where they were, and presumably still are, the standard footwear. It was the custom of the family to take several pairs of these slippers, which had bright red uppers and purple buffalo hide soles, whenever they returned to England. They would become presents for friends and relations.

Enthused, Arthur devised the book not long after he had waved the children off at Windermere station. Collingwood's *Thorstein of the Mere* and its association with Peel Island on Coniston Water came into mind. The initial ideas flourished until he had populated the area with pirates and savages. A draft document written by Ransome, which is now in his immense collection at the Brotherton Library, gives an explanation of "the beginnings" of *Swallows and Amazons.*

Titty and Susan had taken him by surprise at Low Ludderburn – his old cottage under the yews - when

The bank-barn at Low Ludderburn, where Ransome wrote
Swallows and Amazons. He kept his car – "a perambulating
biscuit tin" – in the garage on the left.

The distinctive entrance doors to
the Low Ludderburn bank-barn.

they rushed into the house. Each of the children held a slipper which was enormous, of Syrian style and made of scarlet leather. Ransome, who did not care for crowds, was put out when the other children, and also their father, arrived and reminded him of something he had forgotten. It was his birthday! They would soon be returning to Syria.

In the case of *Swallows and Amazons,* Arthur's usual writing plan – devising chapters, then writing the easiest first – was not followed. The book – from beginning to end – was completed in a single, inspirational surge, his tale being given a contemporary [late twenties] flavour rather than one that was historic. He typed at breakneck speed, using all his fingers. The pen-and-ink drawings that illustrated the book featured children, the images being adapted from photographs of children taken by Arthur.

The Walker children formed the crew of the *Swallow.* Needing a skipper, he turned Tacqui, the eldest child, into a boy named John. The book was dedicated thus: "To the Six for whom it was written, in exchange for a pair of slippers." *Swallows and Amazons* has a distinctive beginning that hints strongly about the theme of the story. Roger, aged seven, traverses a field from lakeside to Holly Howe, where the family are staying. He progresses in broad, boat-like tacks, taking careful note of the breeze. He goes through the motions of anchoring a boat. Mother awaits him. She has a telegram from father, a naval commander in Malta, giving permission for the children to sail to Peel Island. In his reply he observed: "Better drowned than duffers. If duffers – won't drown."

The children, having explored the deserted island, settle into the happy routine of sailing, camping and fishing – until they come under attack from the Amazon Pirates (Nancy and Peggy Blackett), who lived at Beckfoot, and had not only visited the island but claimed that they owned it. Differences were settled in true English style – with an alliance, based on troubling the Blacketts' Uncle Jim, whose temporary residence – while he writes a book – is a houseboat anchored in a quiet bay. Jim is dubbed a pirate - and named Captain Flint! (This grouchy adult might, from his general manner and

Items recovered from the Ransomes' tip at Low Ludderburn.

disposition, be a portrait of Ransome himself!).

When a trunk containing the manuscript of his book and other items is stolen by intruding men, the Captain suspects it is the work of the children – until it is proved otherwise. Peace is restored, but not before Captain Flint is made to walk the plank in true pirate fashion. He provides them with a tasty meal. Ransome ended his book dramatically with a fierce storm. The children resumed their old land-lubbing life and would shortly begin a new year at school, determined to renew their friendship in the following year.

A copy of *Swallows and Amazons* was sent – with a feeling of trepidation – to the Altounyans in Syria. Dora, their mother, who opened the parcel, quickly realised that some of their names had been used. A general impression of their behaviour, as conveyed in the book, was that the children appeared too good to be true. Yet a *Guardian* reviewer noted: "The book is the very stuff of play. It is make-believe such as all children indulge in: even children who have not been so fortunate as to have a lake, a boat and an island but only a backyard amongst the semis of suburbia."

By chance, at Nibthwaite, I was able to chat with Brigit Sanders, née Altounyan, who at the time of the story had been a babe in mother's arms. Now old but with bright eyes, she told me that Ransome had added to their adventures those he remembered from his own young days. "He certainly observed our characters very well, for the children in the book are remarkably close to the actual characters as they were in life." Years after the appearance of *Swallows and Amazons,* Taqui and Titty, having an English education, visited the Ransomes at Low Ludderburn.

Arthur and Evgenia (now often referred to as Genia) had acquired the property on their return to England in the mid-1920s and lived here until the mid-1930s, buying the property for £550, which was £100 less than the original asking price. A lean-to was transformed into a smart kitchen.

Keen to see where the celebrated book was written, I approached Low Ludderburn on a narrow, winding route from the main road in the Lyth Valley which, drained by the Gilpin, consists of large, flat fields with buttressing scars of limestone. These features were well-known to the Ransomes during their Ludderburn years.

The Lyth Valley looks at its most glorious at damson-blossom time. The fruit of trees grown on limestone is especially good. Spending a day in "damson country" in 1968, I saw fruit trees in massed ranks or punctuating the hedges, waiting until the frosts were over before coming wondrously into bloom. Then one had the impression of a sudden fall of snow. On Damson Sunday, the peak of the flowering season, the brilliancy of blossom made the rest of the area look drab.

Lyth Valley is now regarded as a good alternative route to the Windermere area. At Draw Well Farm I chatted with 75-year-old James Edward Inman, whose family had lived hereabouts for about 350 years. He had planted most of the damson trees that stood in attractive battalions. A range of buildings had been built of native stone and slate that had not been knocked about in the interests of modernity. Two cats sunned themselves without fear of sacrificing some of their nine lives – as today - to continuous traffic. A hen strutted, cluckingly, across the byroad. Yes, the Ransomes had been seen passing this way in their old car.

Mr Inman entertained me in a stone-flagged room under an open timber ceiling. We were warmed by a spluttering, aromatic wood fire. I heard that bees living in hives that stood in the orchard at Draw Well Farm were a vital element in the pollination of blossom and that in a normal year the first luscious damsons were being harvested in early September. Mr Inman also remembered years when the first damson pies had been baked in August.

Damsons were despatched from the Valley by the cart and lorry load. Motor vehicles had begun to take over from horses and carts at the end of the First World War. A firm called Ticklers bought a major part of the crop; they needed the damsons for jamming. In the horse-and-cart days, Mr Inman transported damsons from Draw Well to Sandside railway station. On the return trip he counted the other carts, reaching a grand total of 56, with each cart holding about half a ton of fruit.

Turning off the purposeful Lyth Valley road, seeking the Ransome house, led to a feeling of adventure. The narrow road meandered between trees which were in new leaf, giving each view a fresh green background. Eventually, the broad gateway came into view. I walked around yew trees which harboured a brown owl that broke the stillness of Arthur's authorship with its hooting. I then saw with delight what had been the Ransome retreat – a typical small, thick-walled, slate-roofed Lakeland farmhouse, complete with substantial porch to cheat the wind. The place, sheltered from the north by higher ground and trees, overlooked the little-known valley of the Winster.

Ransome had described the farm as a cottage, over three centuries old, perched high on a hillside. Writing in *The Junior Book of Authors*, which was published in 1934, he noted: "I can see forty miles from my cottage door. The lakes I knew best as a boy are close at hand and, on the nearest of them, a little boat, *Swallow*, lies at her moorings and sails as well as ever she did. There is a long row of fishing rods hanging in the cottage, like the pipes of an organ, people say."

The property I saw, newly whitened, contrasted markedly with the dull grey of the bank-barn, its walls two feet thick, which stood just across the yard. At the time the Ransomes lived there, Evgenia cringed at its primitive nature and the dampness that permeated it. The barn had become celebrated because, fitting large windows, Ransome used an upper floor as his workplace. Here, with a clattering typewriter, he wrote *Swallows and Amazons (*also *Peter Duck* and *Winter Holiday)*. The Kelsalls, his neighbours across the valley, were good friends. On writing the early chapters of *Swallows and Amazons*, he would read them to the sons, Desmond and Dick. He was keen to get their reactions. Colonel Kelsall, their father, was also a keen listener.

I stood in a large, high upper room and let my eye stray to one or two reminders of Ransome's residence, notably an elaborate wall-shelf on which a large fish had reposed in a glass case. When the upper floor was Ransome's study, he packed into it books, a mounted pike in a glass cake – and some parrot feathers, a gift from his mother, who thought that some of them might be useful when, as an

Ransome's desk and typewriter in the Ransome Room at Abbot Hall, Kendal. (Museum of Lakeland Life, Kendal)

angler, he was tying flies.

The bank-barn was also the workplace for another feat of writing that began when, in 1925, on a visit to the *Guardian* offices in Manchester, he persuaded Ted Scott that angler readers of the newspaper had nothing specific to read. He was promptly offered a weekly column and a free hand at what it might contain. So while his wife Evgenia kept her eye on the work being done converting the upper floor of the barn into a workplace at their new Lakeland home, Ransome went a-fishing in the waters he recalled as a boy and several others, from the Bowland Hodder to the Cumberland

Ransome at work in
the bank-barn at
Low Ludderburn.
His desk consisted of
two tables pushed
together.
(Brotherton Library,
University of Leeds)

Derwent.

    Standing beside the barn, and almost on the point of collapse, was the garage
where Arthur kept his car, a Morris Cowley, which he likened to "a perambulating
biscuit tin" but enabled him to visit the childhood angling haunts. The situation of
Low Ludderburn, though obscure in the road network of Old Westmorland, suited
Evgenia, who dubbed it the "loveliest spot" in the Lake District. The garden was of
modest size. The views were superb. From a terrace, in clear weather, you might see
Arnside, plus a strip of sea under Arnside Knott, guardian of the Kent estuary.

    Just across the valley was the aforementioned home of Colonel Kelsall, who had recently retired from the Royal Engineers. He was a passionate angler. He and Ransome, living on either side of the little valley, operated a special signalling system, which was the subject of revisions. The code related to aspects of the weather and bearing on the possibility of angling, the times at which they would meet to fish, the availability of bait like minnows and worms. The species mentioned were salmon, white trout, brown trout, grayling, eel and perch.

I was enchanted by the setting. Forty miles away, in another direction, was flat-topped Ingleborough. From the hillside behind the house Arthur revelled in a panoramic view, extending from Black Combe to Helvellyn.

The owner, who had lived here for three decades, laid a grass-strimmer aside and accompanied me into the barn, which is now used for a variety of purposes. There was little that was specifically Ransome, the most prominent being an ornate wooden shelf that appears in an old, somewhat blurred photograph of the author at work. He had a peaceful setting for his writing, which included the work for Ted Scott of the *Manchester Guardian*.

Feathers cast by the family's green parrot were kept, to be used when fishing flies were being fashioned. A rubbish heap at the farm had been cleared, revealing a variety of objects associated with Ransome. Here was a small (broken) teapot and a small bottle that had contained mineral water marketed by Jones Alexander & Sons, Kendal. A small, rectangular bottle sporting the name Foster Clark Ltd/Maidstone had its purpose imposed on the glass. That glass had contained lemonade.

As Ransome had periods of ill-health, I was not surprised to be shown another item recovered from the tip, this being a small bottle with a screw cap that had contained Milk of Magnesia, which had doubtless offered him relief from painful ulcers. A squashed tube of "white vaseline" had been produced and guaranteed by Chesebrough Mfg. Co. Ltd. A bottle holding a dozen or so large, unidentifiable white pills had its neck blocked by cotton wool.

I had visited the Ransome Room at Abbot Hall, Kendal and had seen his desk and typewriter, reminding me of a contribution to *Cumbria* magazine in 1972: "Ransome's plots were straightforward and possible. The adventures of his children were those in which any child could imagine himself playing a part. To these he brought two great gifts – an ability to create character, not by description, but through the speech and actions of his children and adults. However brief and unimportant his part in the plot, each character is whole and rounded and sufficient…"

Ransome's autobiography, with a prologue and epilogue written by his great friend Hart-Davis, gave an insight into a man because, as Hart-Davis noted, Ransome was remarkable in many ways but chiefly because, in himself, there were two different characters. Half of him was a dedicated man of letters, with a passion for language and literature. The other half of him was a perpetual schoolboy, complete with all the zest, fun, enjoyment and enthusiasm of youth.

Both aspects were satisfied when he sat at a desk that was two tables in one and clattered at his ancient typewriter. In an upper room in the old, stone-built barn, he surrounded himself with bits and pieces of sentimental interest – and by a few furnishings that were a gift from Edith, his mother. He was fond of using the old-time pen and ink while writing but in the main the silence was broken by the clattering of his typewriter – which kept pace with his quick thoughts – and, occasionally, the hooting of the local owl.

Writing children's stories satisfied both aspects of the man. Hart-Davis told me that when planning a book, Ransome would jot down a detailed synopsis, complete with chapter titles. Knowing what was going to happen in each chapter, he might choose whichever took his fancy. The most difficult chapters might be left to the last!

Bank Ground Farm was the inspiration for Holly Howe, the summering place of the fictional Walker family. Ernest Altounyan, who married Dora Collingwood, used it as a holiday home. To Arthur, nothing he could write adequately expressed what he owed to "W G Collingwood and his wife, my very dear 'aunt'." Their grandchildren would become the young Walkers, better known as *Swallows,* in the first of his children's books. Sailing in *Amazon,* the rival boat, were the Blackett sisters.

The famous tale involves sailing, angling, swimming and camping under canvas. It is fictional, though based largely on anecdotes concerning the children; it also has an adventurous spirit, the practical base and, to maximise its appeal, a hint of piracy. Arthur had never felt happier than when writing *Swallows and Amazons.* The story would be enacted on an uncharted lake that has affinities with Windermere.

Swallows and Amazons, published when he was

forty-six years of age, would become the first of five children's books with Lakeland settings, the others being *Swallowdale, Winter Holiday, Pigeon Post* and *Picts and Martyrs.* Initially, *Swallows and Amazons* was not illustrated. Then an artist called Clifford Webb was commissioned to provide some pictures. They held a measure of drama but in the end Ransome decided to illustrate the book himself, using a style that implied the artist was a youngster. He was not a brilliant artist, but the style added to the book's charm. He tended to draw his children sideways. This was easier than if they had been presented head-on.

There are, indeed, varying accounts of the genesis of his first *Swallows* book. Take your pick. My favourite has already been outlined. Hugh Brogan, in a footnote to his book about Ransome, stated: "AR wrote at least three different accounts at different stages of his life." One version of how *Swallows and Amazons* came to be written is to be found in Ransome's papers in the Brotherton Library archive at Leeds University. The note, drafted in 1930, dealt with events that took place in 1928.

Summer was spent on the shores of Coniston Water. Ernest, who had been to Walney Island, off Barrow-in-Furness, purchased two seaworthy dinghies. One boat, named Mavis [after a local name for blackbird], was retained. The other, named *Swallow,* passed to Ransome. "It was just then that I thought what fun it would be if I could write them a book about the *Swallow* and the lake and the island that was their playground, as it had been ours, and that of our parents before us."

That, he supposed, was really the beginning of

One of Ransome's original drawings for *Swallows and Amazons*, still carrying dimensions marked up for printing. He found it easier to draw children sideways. (Brotherton Library, University of Leeds)

the book. "I said nothing about it to them, because I did not know whether I should ever be able to write it...a boat cannot do everything in a book. There must be people too, and of course the best possible people would be those very children who had sailed her and given me those slippers."

Writing the book pandered to his love of Lakeland at a time when he had been engaged in an adult world – journalism via the *Manchester Guardian*. "I began to understand that in writing about children one is writing about one's own childhood as well as theirs, and so, in a way, about childhood in general...before I knew what was happening, I was enjoying the writing of the book more than I have enjoyed writing any other book in my life..."

Who, having seen the film version of *Swallows and Amazons*, will forget the spine-tingling sequence in which the children, newly arrived on holiday, race down a field to the lakeside and stare across the lake to a prominent knob of rock given a tufty appearance by a mass of trees? This tree-crowded islet would go down in literary history

The steam yacht *Gondola* provided the initial idea for the houseboat in *Swallows and Amazons*.

as Wild Cat Island.

The children were just old enough to be trusted with boats. The Walkers became Swallows, afloat in a borrowed dinghy. Meanwhile, Nancy and Peggy Blackett took to the lake as Amazons. Here began a well-known spell of rivalry – and an encounter with a pirate, Captain Flint, living on a houseboat. Landlubbers included farmers and charcoal-burners.

Mother, who had brought the children on a lakeside holiday, passed on to him their request to be allowed to sail and camp on Wild Cat Island, which Ransome based partly on Peel Island in Coniston Water. Peel, while having the attractive rock-girt anchorage against which the Walker children brought their dinghy, lacks the size necessary to sustain their antics. The island in the story is more capacious; in the story it has elements of Blakeholme, one of the islands in Windermere.

John, eldest of the Walkers, was – of course – the captain. Susan became the mate and Titty was an

Able Seaman. Young Roger was ship's boy. The *Amazon's* captain was named Nancy Blackett, wih Peggy (her younger sister) as mate. There remained Captain Flint – a name bestowed on James Turner, uncle of the Blacketts.

Nancy and Peggy Blackett, crew of the *Amazon,* were placed in a large house with a lawn leading down to a river. It has been implied that the house may be the one known as Beckfoot; the nearby river flows into Coniston Water. When they sailed in the *Amazon,* the skull and crossbones flag was flown at her masthead and they liked to be known as the Amazon Pirates. In the book, Uncle Jim, who is writing a book, occupies a houseboat moored on the lake, his companion being a parrot. The houseboat is armed with a small cannon. His real name is James Turner. When Titty sees him and his parrot, she concludes he must be a retired pirate.

The Amazon pirates had camped on what they called Wild Cat Island long before the crew of the *Swallow* discovered it. To regain their territory, they make a surprise attack on the Walkers' camp and after a brief skirmish they become allies with the *Swallows* against Uncle Jim, now known as Captain Flint. His houseboat, an idea based on the steam yacht *Gondola,* was eventually modelled on the steam yacht *Esperance* which was built in 1869 for a successful industrialist, H W Schneider, of Belsfield at Bowness.

The houseboat is burgled. Able seaman Titty, having had the good fortune to capture *Amazon,* had it lying at anchor off the rocky island and became aware of where the burglars hid Captain Flint's old cabin trunk. He unjustly suspects the Swallows of

the theft, makes peace when he is proved wrong and is delighted when Titty and Roger between them find the trunk containing his old diaries and the manuscript of his book.

In gratitude, he gives Titty his parrot, but not until he has been made to walk the plank for his misdemeanours. That night there is a thunderstorm. Camping comes to an end. The book closes as the allies part with a promise to meet again. The book was favourably received by his friends but was not an immediate commercial success. This would become one of the most-read children's adventure stories in 1962, when the BBC adapted it for radio, opening with the haunting strains of George Butterworth's *Banks of Green Willow.* It was haunting because the composer had been killed during the Great War. When, eleven years later, EMI adapted the story for the big screen, they resorted to locations in the Lake District that were popularly associated with the tale.

These included Peel Island. Collingwood was fond of recalling this little island for its "pretty little cove for harbour and a well-blackened fire-spot where many a picnic kettle has boiled." Formerly known as Montague Island, after the Lords of the Manor, the island was, as noted, the Wild Cat Island of Ransome's imaginings. Clifford Webb, the artist, had used strong lines to portray it. He pictured a secluded cove, framed by large trees, with upsweeping rock in the background. A sailing dinghy, drawn up on the beach, was being attended by the children.

At the time he devised his first children's book, he was doing most of his fishing and sailing on Windermere, operating from a boatyard at Bowness.

Had he also Ramp Holme in mind for the fictitious Wild Cat Island? Peel Island has its dramatic secret harbour, approached with care to avoid scraping submerged rocks on either shore. On Ramp Holme, rocky outcrops reached out into the lake and a clearing on the raised centre of the island is surrounded by trees. Narrow paths run to the water's edge at various places.

The overall opinion is that Ransome was thinking mainly of Peel Island and this was the main locale for the EMI film version of *Swallows and Amazons.* Ransome had to disguise the place so the participants had a country of their own. He wrote: "No island on Windermere has quite so good a harbour as that among the rocks at the south end of Peel Island on Coniston..."

In the famous tale, John, Susan, Titty and Roger Walker sail a dinghy named *Swallow* to camp on Wild Cat Island and encounter Nancy and Peggy Blackett, pirates operating in a dinghy named *Amazon.* In the tale, the Walkers are staying at a farm near the lake during the school holidays. As, indeed, did the Ransomes. The Blacketts live in a house on the opposite shore. You'll also remember – either from the book or from the film derived from it – their meetings with Captain Flint and his houseboat.

Uncle Arthur's relations with the children continued during a visit the former made to their home in Syria in 1932. There, in the Antioch Lake and the Amuq Marshes, the family re-created their Lakeland activities. And to them, there, Ransome brought *Peter Duck,* a small sailing dinghy. Brigit, then very young, remembered its arrival, "a lovely little boat, clinker built, varnished with a golden

The "pretty little cove for harbour" on Peel Island.

Looking out from Peel Island on a beautiful autumn day.

Coniston Water has three islands. There is Peel Island, which is surely everybody's idea of an island though not large or varied enough to have been a sole inspiration for the fictional Wild Cat Island. It has been suggested that in Ransome's imaginings Peel, on Coniston Water, and Blakeholme, on Windermere, were amalgamated.

At the time *Swallows and Amazons* was published, Ransome was in considerable pain, the cause being diagnosed by his doctor as duodenal or gastric ulcers. He was to write, pithily, in his autobiography: "It so happens that worry stirs up duodenal ulcers, and that ulcers incline their owner to worry." On the day after publication, the pain had increased. Ransome was given a choice between an operation and a long cure. The latter was most appealing. Ransome returned to Windermere. He could not resist writing. Nor fishing in the Leven until, wracked with pain, he returned to his home.

In 1935, tired of living at Low Ludderburn, the Ransomes moved to Suffolk and settled near the River Orwell. In 1940, they moved back to the Lakes, finding a house called Heald. It stood on the shore of Coniston Water. Arthur found it harder to keep writing. *Picts and Martyrs* was published in 1943. The last of the *Swallows and Amazons* series appeared in 1947. His wife, a restless soul, showed no pleasure in his books. The Ransomes had badly wanted to have children of their own. In the end they had to be content with his fictional children.

colour." She recalled seeing "Uncle Arthur" catch a catfish from a bridge in the marsh. He had promptly described it, for her benefit, as a fearsome monster which leapt out of the water and barked at him, evidence of his intuitive awareness of the fantasy world which is part of a child's reality.

Ransome and his wife came to view the Syrian family with less friendly eyes as time went by. Arthur's wife, in particular, seemed anxious to reject any suggestion that the famous stories (whose writing she had always opposed and criticised ruthlessly) were based on the Altounyan children. The facts, however, speak for themselves.

Steamboats Ruled the Waves

From boyhood, Ransome found pleasure in the sight, on Coniston Water or Windermere, of a plume of white smoke, signifying the presence of a steamboat. Sailing dinghies took precedence in his stories but, to him, steamers were as much a part of the Lakeland backdrop as trees and fells.

Ransome, in his autobiography, incomplete at the time of his death, and published during my editorship of *Cumbria* magazine, joyfully referred to an elegant steam-yacht named *Gondola*, built for the Coniston Railway Company and launched in 1859,

the year in which the railway was open for traffic.

Gondola, fashioned of Low Moor iron, had been assembled on the lakeside near Coniston Hall. Described as "the perfect combination of the Venetian gondola and the English steam yacht", it operated a regular service during the tourist season of 1860. In *Swallows and Amazons*, Ransome was to base Captain Flint's houseboat partly on *Gondola* and partly on *Esperance*, which cruised on Windermere and is now in the Windermere Steamboat Museum.

Gondola, **photographed in 1906 when it had already been operating on Coniston Water for forty-six years.**

The fully restored *Gondola*, which once again carries passengers on the lake. Clearly visible on the prow is the carved snake's head with fangs outstretched.

Gondola operated between Waterhead pier at Coniston and the jetty at Lake Bank from the middle of May to the end of September. Felix Hamill, its captain, was one of Ransome's local heroes. Hamill was described by a friend as being a tidy man with a rather dense beard and a serious look on his face. Hamill's pride in the *Gondola* was the driving force in his life for nearly fifty years. He permitted the young Ransome to steer "his noble vessel", standing behind him at an iron wheel with six spokes that was set above the engine room. When for the last time in the year, the steam yacht left the pier at Lake Bank, the captain sounded his whistle, giving Arthur an enduring memory of "a long last wail of farewell...It always rained on that day, both indoors and out of doors."

A Nibthwaite lady recalled that at the prow of the *Gondola* was a carved snake's head, with fangs outstretched, fixed above a gilded crown and the full coat of arms of the Duke of Devonshire, chairman of the Furness Railway. On the stern-counter were the alms of the Duke of Buccleuch, who owned the lake. These and many other items, such as the seat-ends carved with acanthus leaves, and the doors of the saloon, were preserved and restored. The craft's original design had been faulty. A standard type of funnel was upright. *Gondola* was fitted with a funnel set horizontally, so that smoke and fumes might be emitted at the stern. As the new-style craft entered Coniston Water with a full head of steam, water flowed up the funnel – and put out the boiler fire!

The customary vertical type of funnel was installed.

Gondola served Coniston Water for about 80 years. The topographer W T Palmer considered that her shape was strange. At the stern, where the engines were placed, the draught was a yard and a-half, tapering to nothing at the gradually rising bow. Ransome was doubtless amused at such a place to see passengers disembark by ladder from the bow on to dry land. The arrangement of the cabin was unique. The ribs of the hull continued upwards between the windows and curved over in the form of complete iron hoops to support the cabin roof. When the saloon doors fore and aft were closed, the crew might walk from stem to stern along foot-wide bulwarks outside the cabin on both sides of the vessel. They were supported by curved wrought-iron brackets bolted to the topside of the hull.

Captain Hamill completed over 13,000 sailings,

in all weathers, with scarcely a scratch. A family man, he raised nine offspring, his quaint home lying above the waiting room of the boathouse at Waterhead pier. In winter, *Gondola* was stored – as far as her funnel – in a boathouse beneath the house! In 1908, *The Lady of the Lake* was constructed to replace her. Yet both craft were operated and it was *Lady,* not *Gondola,* that was scrapped in 1950. Everyone except John Ruskin enthused about the *Gondola.* Ruskin had an aversion to steam, especially steam locomotives running on rails. Yet once, boarding *Gondola* for a voyage to Lake Bank, he was so delighted on being shown over the boat he remarked to Captain Hamill: "I *may* like steam after all."

Brigit Sanders, a granddaughter of W G Collingwood, whom I met at Nibthwaite, told me of the elegance of the craft. Captain Hamill appeared to the passengers as a dapper little man, wearing a black peaked cap. Robert Wilkinson, a resident of Coniston for nearly eighty years – and son of Miles, gardener at Brantwood – recalled Sunday school outings. Captain Hamill was "a really grand old chap", though he had a disconcerting habit of chasing young anglers from the Waterhead pier at Coniston.

Esperance, afloat on Windermere, was engineless at the time when Ransome knew her. When I was invited to cruise in her, she was in lakeworthy condition. As a houseboat in *Swallows and Amazons,* she had served as houseboat to the Blackett girls' Uncle Jim. He was classified as a pirate. On my visit to *Esperance,* a stuffed parrot occupied one of the window spaces. The craft's neat and perfect design had been preserved by George Pattinson, her owner, whose family had owned the craft since 1941. With a length of 75 feet long, she had a brown superstructure and a slim black funnel to accentuate her neat lines.

George recalled several meetings with Arthur Ransome and also one of the spectacular wartime sights of Windermere that would have appealed to him. I refer to the assembly of Short Sunderland flying-boats using parts that had been produced in various centres of Britain. They were flown off the lake and into service. One of the lake steamers became a Royal Navy vessel for the duration. George's father, invited by one of the Short brothers to join a test flight, was asked where he would like to be taken. He mentioned owning some land in Great Langdale, so the aircraft was flown in that direction. Its size and the noise of its four engines no doubt put all the local hens off the lay for days on end.

As her proud owner demonstrated her capabilities on the lake, the raked stem of *Esperance* took the spirit out of wavelets created by a gusty wind. The original engines had been of a compound type with a single cylinder block and two sets of inclined pistons, forming an inverted V, with connecting rods going down to each shaft. The heart of the "old lady" still beat strongly, though she was powered by petrol instead of steam. The funnel took exhaust fumes from two 4-cylinder Ford engines that combined to yield 49 hp. A device for producing steam added a touch of realism.

Esperance was so perfectly designed, with tapering hull and graceful counter, that she might be towed from a rowing boat. Indeed, it was in such a boat that George Pattinson rowed me out to her

Esperance, the 'grand old lady of Windermere', moored at the Bowness Steamboat Museum.

Raven, another early Windermere steamer at the Steamboat Museum.

moorings. Unrestrained, and with only one engine ticking over, he took me for a mini-cruise, coming close inshore at Bowness Bay – the Rio of Ransome's imaginings. I was shown the pier against which *Esperance* was moored during her early years. The pier is still named after the craft.

Esperance had an amazingly varied career since she was built by T H Seath and Company of Rutherglen in 1869. The craft belonged to H W Schneider, a notable industrialist. Belsfield, adjacent to Bowness Bay, was Schneider's residence from 1869 until his death in 1887, since when it has been a hotel for many years. George Pattinson had a painting of the building as it was in Schneider's day. The artist portrayed the slim little *Esperance* moored to its pier.

Each weekday morning, Schneider had walked to the pier, preceded – it is said – by his butler, who carried his breakfast on a silver tray. There was a crew of two men. The proud owner dined twixt home and the terminal at Lakeside, a distance of seven miles that was covered in less than an hour. He boarded a special train and was taken to Barrow-in-Furness, where he presided over his business affairs.

After the death of Schneider, *Esperance* was left high and dry, having been hauled out of the water south of Cockshott Point. Four years elapsed before she was operating again. Bought by Mr Logan, of the *Ferry Hotel*, on the Lancashire shore of Windermere, she ferried passengers between the hotel and Bowness, a course now taken by the ferry. Guests at the *Ferry Hotel* boarded her to attend church at Wray.

In the later 1930s, *Esperance* – always thought of by local people as "the old lady of the lake" - was forlorn and almost forgotten. She lay on the bed of the lake where there was twenty feet of water. Ransome, keen angler, frequenter of the waterside, undoubtedly saw her in this distressful state. George Pattinson's father had her raised from her muddy bed. It saddened him to think of her underwater fate.

When, after my mini-cruise, the *Esperance* was at its moorings in Rayrigg Bay I was entertained to tea in the forward saloon. Then, in the after saloon, I admired photographs of other notable Windermere steamers including *Fairy Queen,* owned by Col G J M Ridehalgh, of Fell Foot. The boat was lit by gas, manufactured on board. Col Ridehalgh's second steamer, the *Britannia,* stirred the water of Windermere in 1880 and was bought by the Furness Railway Company in 1907 for £350. Withdrawn from service in 1915, she was broken up in 1919.

When Arthur Ransome and Evgenia lived at Low Ludderburn near Windermere, they sailed on the lake in their much-prized dinghy named *Swallow.* Sailing and fishing were continuous pleasures. Angling observations and experiences were

Ransome's much-prized boat at the Bowness Steamboat Museum.

entertainingly recorded in his column in the *Manchester Guardian.* Daughter Tabitha was invited to join the Ransomes on a sailing holiday, but her neurotic mother objected. She affirmed that if Tabitha went to Windermere, her father would surely drown her!

Four motor vessels operated a passenger service twixt Lakeside and Waterhead. The sleek, white-hulled craft were beginning their 101st season amid the glitter of celebrations, the service having begun in Furness Railway days. A lease for the service was necessary, the bed of the lake being owned by Windermere Urban District Council, to whom it was presented by Alderman H Leigh Groves.

Six years after the publication of *Swallows and Amazons,* there was a tremor of excitement on Windermere with the introduction of two new steamers – *Teal* and *Swan.* In each case, they were the second craft to bear the name locally. Both vessels, looming high from the water and having a shallow draught, offered a broad and tempting surface to a frolicsome wind.

In 1964, I paid my respects to one of the "big white birds". I chose the good ship *Teal,* which had William McGarr as its captain. It was his first season in charge of *Teal.* He had served as captain on other craft for twelve years and was mate on the *Teal* for a spell. For six summers in the 1930s – *Swallows and Amazons* time, doubtless with Ransome as an occasional passenger – he had been a humble deckhand. I joined her at Lakeside. Half-power was employed until she cleared the rowing boats at the *Lakeside Hotel.* Reaching for the telegraph, Captain McGarr signalled "full ahead" on both engines.

The speed of the screws quickened as Gleniffer diesel engines, each generating 160 hp, responded to the summons, drinking in the first of about 50 gallons of fuel they would consume before nightfall. Cruising at ten and a-half knots, *Teal* had the lake to itself. And, beholding the Windermere shoreline from a novel angle, I could think of Ransome connections with England's largest lake.

Looking astern, beyond the "red duster" that slapped itself in a stiff breeze, I saw a broad wake flecked by sunlight and the yellow-painted terminus at Lakeside. Ransome would recall seeing heaps of coal, intended to be burnt to keep the screws of the vessels turning. At night, quayside coal stocks were replenished. A single boat might need about 30 swills [large baskets] of coal, each swill holding a hundredweight. In dry weather, coal dust blew everywhere.

Large houses, never properly seen by road users, stood in their well-tended grounds, smacked by a lake that as a result of torrential rain was three feet above its summertime normal of 128 feet 3 inches. The Westmorland local government authority had claimed the area at Lakeside on which the steamer terminus was built, the land having been reclaimed from the bed of the lake. It was then surrounded on three sides by Lancashire. The cinema film of *Swallows and Amazons* began with a steam train on the track for Lakeside. Roger was already fantasising about the landscape and its wild creatures (mainly cows) that he viewed from the large windows.

On my steamer trip, as Storrs approached, the captain was aware of the shallows. They were well-buoyed, especially the notorious Oven Bottom. Up to 1935, the steamers – as they were – stopped at the Storrs and Lowwood piers by request. Another halt had been *Ferry Hotel,* which was subsequently the headquarters of the Freshwater Biological Association.

It was at the approach to Bowness Bay that the greatest concentration was needed by Captain McGarr and Ronald Backhouse, the helmsman. Windermere-type racing yachts were moored just outside the bay. Rowing boats and self-drive hire motor boats moved about like varnished water beetles. The direction of the wind was studied. A decision was reached as to which side of the pier would be used. *Teal* nudged the pier and was tied up.

When Bowness Bay lay astern, the mate relieved the skipper on the bridge. Below decks, I was told about the British Railways fleet. Ransome would have been able, adroitly, to work some of them into his stories. A ticket collector had asked a passenger if he was a first-class passenger, to be told: "I is, my lad; but I don't ken thoo." A woman who had temporarily lost her husband was advised to return to the point where she had embarked. A helpful boatman asked her to describe it. Said she: "It had got a pier. And there were trees and water."

After the low, rounded Silurian hills of Windermere, the head of the lake had a grand backdrop in the loftier, starker, well-grouped fells of the Borrowdale Volcanics. As the boat approached Waterhead, my attention was claimed by Fairfield, Loughrigg, the Langdale Pikes and the solemn grandeur of the skyline beyond Coniston.

Coal, boilers and funnels had long since given way to engines fuelled by diesel oil. Robert Casson, engineer on the *Swan,* was the proud owner of the old steam whistle from the *Tern.* In the mid-19th century, there were two rival companies. The Furness Railway had bought the service in 1871 – about the time the aforementioned *Esperance* was launched.

These "big white birds" of Windermere were in 1972 available for charter. A family had called at Lakeside to arrange a charter. When all the details were explained to them, one of the visitors ruefully admitted that they wished to charter a rowing boat! A lady tried the patience of the staff when she sat on the boat at Waterhead and insisted on being taken direct to Barrow-in-Furness.

Several times it was explained that the steamer went to Lakeside only. She would have to take a bus from the eastern side of the lake. "But it says it goes to Barrow," she insisted and, taking the officials round to the stern she pointed to the vessel's name and port of registration – Barrow!

Swift, built in 1900 and long the largest of the old steam fleet on Windermere, would be familiar to the Ransomes.

The distinctive prow of *Tern,* launched in 1891 and still surviving as the flagship of the Windermere fleet.

Ransome enjoyed fishing on Windermere when there were no "monstrous and noisy" motor boats. He would have appreciated this tranquil scene at Bowness Bay.

Arthur the Angler

Arthur enjoyed fishing but never claimed to be a good angler. He had found pleasure in salmon fishing from the bank of a stream or when sitting on a wicker basket with other anglers on a canal towpath. Fishing was in his blood for he was the third generation of his family to delight in rod and line. Given a choice, his grandfather would settle down beside the Bela, to the south of the Lake District.

Ransome first fished the Bela in 1930 and, when chatting to an old keeper who had been appointed by the club controlling the angling, heard one of grandfather's tales of sixty years before. A member of the club committee had queried what was to be done about a superannuation fund. Grandfather had snorted that no-one appointed keeper on that river would want to be superannuated. The keeper never had – and never would – ask to be superannuated.

When Ransome's father was in a dream-like state, pondering on his favourite angling haunts, and of the brown trout that was his favourite quarry, he would recall jaunts to the Bela, also to Coniston Water, on the banks of which the Ransome family spent the Long Vacation.

In the early days, when father was giving him instruction in angling by the mighty Wharfe, Arthur was inclined to dodge some of the lessons, sneaking to a lower reach of the river, here to catch loaches. At Coniston, he had his own rod and could seek perch with a chance of catching some equal to those of his dad.

Arthur considered that the Bela was a model river, though his inaugural experiences came when he observed his father catching trout on the River Wharfe, just over the hill from the family home in Leeds. The roles were those of master and pupil. In Lakeland, father seemed to change from a professor who fished to a fisherman with a spare-time interest in history

Angling as well as tale-telling was to keep the keys of Ransome's typewriter clacking. Fishing was a feature of many a book, including *Swallows and Amazons*, where Captain Flint imparts to them some of his practical knowledge of hooking perch in the lake, the bait being minnows. (In one case, a pike left its mark on the dead perch that was captured). Beck trout made their debut in *Swallowdale.*

In later days, he shuddered when, with warm weather towards the end of April, motor-boats appeared on Windermere. When fishing should be good, the monstrous and noisy boats roared up and down the lake, leaving films of oil on the water. He was inclined to seek remoter, less fishable lakes that were nonetheless free from motor boats.

As noted, Ransome did not claim to be a good fisherman, only one who thoroughly enjoyed the sport. Fishing with rod and line was not for Young Arthur, who initially paddled in the water and, turning stones, caught loaches. When fishing by Coniston Water, he wielded a rod of his own and had an almost equal chance with his father of catching perch. *Otley's Guide to the Lakes* (1814) listed perch, along with char, trout, pike and eels. Father kept his rod leaning against the porch at Swainsons' farm. The young folk were encouraged to play near the boathouse – and "watch for the fish to rise!"

Father died in 1897. Arthur laid down his rod and did not pick it up again until the summer of 1910.The man who reintroduced him to angling was a postman friend at Milford by Godalming, who persuaded him to try fishing on the Wey. He caught two roach – pleasurably. Not only angling came into his accounts of how to catch fish. There was the old Lakeland trout-tickling routine which was known, in the local dialect, as *guddling*. Jacky, a character in *The Picts and the Martyrs,* had indicated that you must keep *guddling* and *guddling* until your fingers were round the middle of the fish. Avoid touching the tail. Under these circumstances, the trout would "lig quiet" until grabbed.

At the time of the Eclipse of the Sun (29 June, 1927), Ransome visited Malham Tarn, which laps and frets on a hard base in the limestone country of Craven. He was keen to study the likely effect of the Eclipse on fish. After all, at such a time cattle were known to stop feeding. Birds made a premature return to their roosts. In his book *Rod and Line* he thought that fish might show their interest by swimming at the top of the water – that at 6.24 a.m. there would be a conspicuous Evening Rise.

He left the dale and its crowd of excited Eclipse-watchers, their chatter, mouth organs, accordions and a brass band. Breaking a rule, he was at the tarnside at 5.30. When a flock of geese had noisily departed, he revelled in the peacefulness. A light wind strummed the water. He prepared his tackle as if he was responding to an Evening Rise and then drifted in a rowing boat, occasionally pulling on the oars. At Eclipse time, darkness covered the face of land and water and there was silence, even among the moor birds.

Ransome was less interested in "the shrouded sun" than in the behaviour of the fish. The tarn was dead, with no hint that the fish were rising. He had the impression that to them it was a tremendous shadow, not of a cloud but of a solid body. Their response was as it might have been if the shadow of an angler or his tackle fell on the water, burying themselves in the weeds or deepest water.

When daylight returned, twenty minutes elapsed before Ransome saw the first fish rise. Drifting down on him, and getting his flies over him, he bagged the trout, which was just over the limit. Soon afterwards he had hooked another trout which, being under the limit, was returned to the tarn. His morning's fishing was "ordinary" and "one of the worst". The reactions of fish were disappointing, being "entirely negative".

Rupert Hart-Davis, who went on a fishing trip with him, recalled with amusement the day they sought pike, pointing out to Arthur a large black cloud that was rolling up. His reply was "don't worry, dear boy". He had known the area for a long time. No trouble ever came from that direction. They carried on pike fishing. A great storm broke. Fishing was abandoned for the day.

Judging by his written work, he was at his angling best when writing about the Lakeland waters he loved. His book *Mainly about Fishing* was published in 1959 and his angling earned a place in literature for his accounts of fishing for perch in the lake in *Swallows and Amazons* and for the trout frequenting Lakeland tarns, as in *Swallowdale.*

His first opportunity for fishing had come by Coniston Water. Young Arthur had a rod of his own. His chances of catching perch equalled those of his father who during a long vacation might forget his university professorship and the books he penned in his spare time, concentrating on angling. He taught his son how to handle a sailing boat.

Ransome was over sixty years of age before he landed a prize fish, this being a twenty-pound salmon. His biggest brown trout, caught in 1955, made the scales dip at only 3¼ lb. A year later he landed his largest sea trout, at 5½ lb. As regards shooting, he was nearly sixty years of age, and father was dead, when Arthur graduated to carrying a loaded shotgun in the great outdoors.

When he and Evgenia were living at Low Ludderburn he was in frequent contact, across the broad valley of the Winster, with Colonel Kelsall, of Barkbooth. Ransome was to incorporate in *Swallowdale,* the longest of his children's books, the aforementioned signalling code that he and Colonel Kelsall had evolved to avoid a long car run between houses. As Ransome wryly observed, the fish did not have advanced warning of what was to befall them. The signals displayed varied in shape, four shapes indeed, lettered A to D – A being represented by a diamond; B by a square; C triangle, main point upwards; D triangle, inverted. Each represented a current practical thought about angling possibilities.

Being somewhat military in style, it is more than likely that the Colonel devised them. At the Leeds archive I was to see the following:

1. A. *Answer.* 2. B. *Shall we fish today?* 3. C. *Yes.* 4. D. *No.* 5. A.C. *I am coming to see you.* 6. A.D. *Have you any minnows?* 7. B.C. *Weather doubtful.* 8. B.D. *Will you come to tea?* 9. C.A. *Shall we fish tomorrow?* 10. C.B. *Flag wag ?!!!!! Impossible.* 11. D.A. *Weather good.* 12. D.B. *Weather bad.*

At the lakeside, Coniston, in 1972, I chatted with Robert Clarke, one of two men who made rowing boats available to visitors. Robert had served his time to boat building with Borwicks of Bowness Bay. We discussed Arthur Ransome and angling. Robert asserted that in Coniston Water and Windermere the most suitable bait was live minnow. He added: "If a man gets the char bug, he'll cut up a gold watch for bait". A watchcase, shimmering deep in the lake, was an effective lure for char. He considered this species "a lovely fish to eat. To me, they taste as good as salmon."

In the 1980s, I chatted with some of the men who fished for salmon and trout in the Crake Valley. I was told that the river Crake is tidal as far as Little Dick's Farm. One of my informants, Mr Satterthwaite, a local fisherman for half a century, recalled that during the 1939-45 war, at the instigation of the Ministry of Agriculture, he ran an eel trap to augment the scarce food supplies.

Students from Wray Castle, where the Freshwater Biological Association was based, helped him with the enterprise. Lights were strung above the weir to "turn" the eels to where the trap, a wooden box with slatted floor, awaited them. "We used to start about

The deep pools of the River Crake, holding fish even in a dry summer, were undoubtedly known to Ransome.

Char on the menu at a Windermere café.

A magnificent cock salmon.

Char-fishing tackle at Bowness.

Sailing boat on Coniston Water. It was joyful discovery to Ransome when he found he could catch char from such a craft.

July or August on the first dark, wild and windy night. The eggs had changed to silver and looked most attractive."

Everyone I met, twenty years ago, commented on the scarcity of salmon. Mr Satterthwaite had hooked a fish weighing 16 lb but mostly they weighed from 7lb to 10lb. The sea trout were usually caught at night. Individuals weighed between 1lb and 3lb. At Spark Bridge, Jock Buchanan, who as his name implied was a Scotsman, found a wife hereabouts and for the past quarter of a century they had lived within sight and hearing of the river. He confirmed my impression that salmon disease caused the initial decline of the fishery. The final straw was when poachers "cymagged" the water on two occasions. A vast number of fish had died.

Jock looked back with joy on the day he hooked seven salmon while fishing the Garden Hole – virtually at the bottom of his garden. His mother-in-law, a keen angler, had the fishing rights in that "lie" and so permission to fish was readily forthcoming. The Garden Hole, which was undoubtedly known to Arthur Ransome, was then the deepest pool on the river, holding some fish even in a dry summer.

Jock told me of the peculiar pleasures of night-fishing for sea trout and of how a bat alighted on the tip of a friend's rod, to his great surprise. The fishing rights in the Crake were once owned by the old Major – Ulf Machell, of Penny Bridge Hall.

Char fishing was possible only in June and September, "when char come up from the deeps."

I looked in vain for any detailed references to char, which occur in the chilly depths of both Coniston Water and Windermere, but – demanding specialist tackle to catch them – they were initially out of Ransome's reach. He contented himself by hooking trout, perch and pike.

In a letter to his mother, in later life, quoted by Hugh Brogan, Ransome recalled a joyful discovery – that although he was not capable of rowing a boat, he might catch a char by sailing. (It was a method based on the tunny fishers of the Bay of Biscay!). One must sail slowly. Hooking a fish at a range of sixty to eighty miles was relatively easy; the complex part was combining the tasks of handling sail, rudder, rod, reel and net "with only two hands and false teeth".

The char, *salvelinus alpinus,* a member of the salmon family, has a circumpolar distribution. In some countries, the fish is migratory. It hatches in fresh water but the young fish migrate to feed in the sea, returning to freshwater, usually the river of their birth, to breed. I had an illuminating chat with Dr Winifred Frost, of the Freshwater Biological Association, based on the former Ferry House; she was an authority on the biology of Windermere char.

They had become landlocked, presumably at the end of the Ice Age, around 14,000 years ago. A typical char is 10 to 12 inches long. The belly of a breeding male assumes a brilliant orange-red colour and white edges to the fins have an enamel-like intensity. The breeding female has a "spawning dress" that is less bright, though both have olive-green backs.

Lake District char feed and breed in freshwater, the main food being a small crustacean – a water flea called collectively Cladocera (having a resemblance in size and shape to the char fisherman's most attractive lure!). Dr Frost mentioned there are two different populations of char in Windermere; they are separated by their breeding habits, one population spawning in November in shallow water, the other in mid-February and March in deep water.

The fishing season extends from March to September. The method of fishing for char would fascinate Ransome because it was so different from normal techniques. The technique varies subtly from fisherman to fisherman. The fish was trolled from a boat, which must be strong enough to withstand wind and weather on this large lake.

The rod, for which a special rest is screwed on to the side of the boat, is 15 feet long, traditionally made of ash. There are, indeed, two rods, extending from the boat at angles of 45 degrees. The main line of 90 feet is attached to the rod with a series of half-hitches or simply fastened to the end of it with a metal clip. A bell, attached to the end of the rod, warns the angler of a catch. Now the tip of a rod might go under water. A long line, weighted at the end, extended downwards. Lines spaced at 10 to 12 feet went off horizontally. These were "tail lines", attached to the bait. Years ago, the bait consisted of live minnows. Lately, there was a spinner, to which was attached a treble hook.

In a New Edition of Collingwood's *The Lake Counties,* dating from the early 1930s, a fishing section is contributed by A. Severn, who gives much practical information and also enchants with its presentation, such as: "During a flood the streams look like dark coffee, while the foam is the colour of sherry. As long as the spate lasts it would seem that all the trout must be washed away; yet the same stream which when dead low appeared to have very few fish in it is now alive with them – as though they had been hiding in the heather waiting for the rain."

The angler could expect these "mountain trout" to be very small, their growth restricted by the scarcity of food, "a single thunder shower being enough to wash away in a few moments what food has been formed on the mossy rocks. In a fairly large-sized beck there is always the possibility of catching some good lake fish if there have been no serious obstructions to prevent their running up, but as soon as the water runs down they will find their way back to the lake."

Climbing t'Old Man

The Old Man of Coniston, west of Coniston Water, was part of Ransome's favourite boyhood view. It was to Coniston village what the Matterhorn was to Zermatt in Switzerland. Ransome dubbed the Old Man 'Kanchenjunga' in *Swallowdale,* which was the 1931 follow-up to *Swallows and Amazons.* In Ransome's time, the Lake District was shared by three counties – Cumberland, Westmorland and Lancashire North of the Sands. They met at the head of Wrynose Pass. When Ransome's fictional children climbed Kanchenjunga they never left Lancashire.

Despite its links with mining and quarrying, the Old Man is a fell in the Lakeland tradition, consisting of hard-wearing rock of the Borrowdale volcanic series, through crags giving it a knobbly topography. It was the industrial archaeologist's favourite mountain. Coppermines Valley in particular holds a fascination for anyone whose

Coniston Old Man is prominent on the skyline in this lakeside view at Nibthwaite.

interests lie in this direction. Here are ruins and rusted artefacts.

I approached Coniston via birch woods. The trees stood in new grass a foot deep. Hillside glowed with flowering gorse. Blackthorn blossom was thick enough to be taken for snow. California poppies (yellow) festooned the roadside. In the fields were Herdwick sheep, mostly with black lambs. The Old Man of Coniston was cloud-capped. I marked the start of my expedition with a pint of Old Man ale.

Motoring from the village up the Walna Scar road enabled me to gain 750-ft without perspiring. The road was narrow, winding and steep. Happily, I had the tarmac to myself. Having parked the car, I trudged along the road to where a quarry track led to the heights and, at the bottom, a large chunk of slate had a white arrow on it and the words: "Path to Old Man". Coniston slate is of light and dark greys. There is also a blue-grey.

I climbed steadily, between expanses of bracken, most of which was unfolding, each frond having a curved top, like a bishop's crozier. Meadow

Working conditions and equipment at the Coniston copper mines would be similar to this scene re-created in the Mining Museum at Threlkeld.

pipits, singing, were in shuttlecock flight, wings and tails held stiffly outwards. Coniston Water was gunmetal grey under cloud. Where the ground was spangled by tormentil, the path bifurcated.

I bore to the left, on what was the scenic route. More steady tramping, interspersed with stops to view the lake and fells. A black slug moved steadily uphill (giving me the fanciful thought of it taking a year or two to reach the summit, hibernating in winter). More slugs were seen. One had curled up, as though for a nap. I moved confidently, along the wrong path.

The famous scenic view was no more. Old Man had a hood of cloud. Higher up, I felt a wind with an edge to it like a knife. Then, joyfully, I was at the summit, paying homage to an immense cairn, set on a gigantic slate foundation, complete with steps, and keeping an eye on a sheep which in turn had its eyes on the rucksack I had temporarily discarded. A lesser black-backed gull was perched on the trig point. Clouds played hide and seek around the striated crags of Dow. I enjoyed a view of Low Water as sunlight made it sparkle.

W G Collingwood, friend of Arthur Ransome, wrote that in spite of various guesses as to the meaning, the name Old Man is probably nothing more nor less than the old cairn on the highest of Coniston Fells. "The present cairn was made by the Ordnance Surveyors; before that there were three ancient stone heaps - 'the old man, his wife, and his son'...In spite of mines and quarries and watercourses, this labyrinth of coves and crags is impressive mountain scenery..."

Another time, I climbed by the more popular route that I dubbed Ransome Way, via Church Beck and the copper mines. It is believed that Romans first tickled the slaty ribs of t'Old Man looking for minerals. The quest intensified between 1850 and 1870. On previous visits I heard the clink of slate at every footfall and was awestruck by the fact that miners worked to a depth of up to 1,100ft, many of their systems being now waterlogged.

My late friend, A H Griffin, wrote that one of Ransome's most interesting distinctions was that he was probably the youngest person to reach the summit of the Old Man. He was only a few weeks old. As related, Arthur's father had been disappointed that the birth of his son had occurred during term time; he narrowly missed being born a Lakelander. So to make up for it, he carried Baby Arthur to the top of what was then the highest mountain in Lancashire North of the Sands.

On a visit to the Old Man in the summer of 1952, I first chatted with an old lady in a cottage at a time when two brass candlesticks on the mantelpiece blinked in strong sunlight. Just below them, a kettle sang quietly to itself, held in place by a hook on a well-polished reckan. The old lady walked to the sideboard and returned with a thin strip of metal – a common metal, of no great value. The smile on her face and tone of voice suggested that, to her, it was a treasure. A piece of copper – mined at Coniston.

Copper was extracted from the local fells until the 1914-18 war. George Stephens, aged 82, told me that the old-time copper-workers were paid at the rate of a guinea a week. When he started at the mines, aged eleven, his weekly pay was 4s. John Thwaite, who lived at one of a row of mining houses, had been a slate-splitter at quarries on the Old Man. He started work at the age of thirteen and earned 1s a working day, which began at 7 a.m and ended at 5.30 p.m. He had earned 6d a day picking copper when it was brought to the surface. The closure of the mines led to the presence of many empty houses. Most workers emigrated to the industrial parts of what was then known as Cumberland.

I walked along a quiet road that soon became a track, littered with green slate that tinkled musically underfoot. The local sheep stopped grazing and watched me with interest rather than anxiety. The path twisted as it climbed. Church Beck roared in its ravine. Successive torrents had carved fantastic patterns in the rock.

At 700-ft above sea level, high above the grey strip that was Coniston Water under cloud, I saw old copper workings. Across the valley floor were the stumps of buildings and heaps of debris. The mines had eventually extended from Brim Fell top, up Red Dell, under Wetherlam and over by Tilberthwaite into Little Langdale.

Bill Shaw, a native of Coniston who I met at Keswick in 1973, knew as much, if not more, about the mines than anyone else. He wrote a book entitled *Mining in the Lake Counties.* Coniston was best-known, perhaps, for its ancient copper mines. There were ripples of excitement about copper mines when Bill was a boy in the village. No one could personally remember the great days of the mines prior to the middle of the 19th century, after which time the price of copper fell away to about £30 a ton and the work stopped. He could remember when a French

company operated there.

Said Bill: "They came before the 1914-18 war, intending to open the mines in a big way. First, however, they were to work through the old mine dumps. The plant was said to cost £30,000. My father came back into the district to help with the work. It never came to anything. The last underground mining was in 1908. Local people were left with memories of seeing Count Henri de Varnie, the engineer – a rare person in those days, having the ability to fly an aircraft. When the Great War started he was called up into the French Air Force, was shot down – and died."

Count Henri stayed at the *Waterhead Hotel,* the main hostelry in Coniston. When Bill was a boy of about five, his family was living across the lake from Coniston. He remembered being taken up to the mines and seeing this romantic French count. Bill remembered even more when a chimney was smoking at the smelter – and dirty water flowed down the beck from the crushing mill.

The last attempt to open up the copper mines came in the mid-1950s, when the price of copper was good. Before anything could be developed, that price had tumbled again, this time to below £300 a ton. Bill believed there is a good deal of copper left. "I have never seen it, but the old people told me this was so."

Was there gold in them-thar hills? There is a little gold in the copper ore. The Germans obtained some from Coniston and Newlands. One might find gold with difficulty and protracted effort. The income from its sale would hardly cover wear and tear of clothes and boots.

Farmers and Sportsmen

Ransome's life in the Lake District was enhanced by angling and also by such hardy annual events as hound-trailing and wrestling. He rejoiced in their strong Lakeland background. There were major events like Grasmere Sports and less formal gatherings such as Shepherds' Meets, when stray sheep in the different areas were sorted and returned to their owners. I have no record of him attending a Merry Neet, which was a time for boozing and singing. He found space in *Swallowdale* – the longest of his books – to deal with life set against a rocky terrain, a grey, weepy climate and a long, long winter. In the Lake District there was no permanent snow cover, yet snow might powder the "tops" over 2,500-ft on a hundred days in the year.
My experiences of Lakeland farmers go back to Ransome Time. Fell farms in the upper dales contrasted with lile farmsteads, many such holdings being found in Furness, the area he knew best. When angling, he would have to cross someone else's land to reach the waterside. A Lakeland farmer was likely to think of himself as t'boss, though it was his wife – often the most dynamic of the duo – who held the family and the farm together.

Ransome would be familiar with a farmer's working garb – flat tweed cap, a Union shirt made of heavy cotton with a neck-band but no collar, and knee-breeches worn in conjunction with leather gaiters or ankle-straps. Away from the farm, in the warmer months of the year, a farmer would don a *kitle*, a coat that was light and durable fabric. There would be a pocket for *bacca* [tobacco] for either smoking or chewing. And mints, of course. The earthy farm tang was off-set by the flavour of mints!

In his young days, Ransome joined a group of local lads who were keen on wrestling, Cumberland and Westmorland style. They practised their sport in the evening, aiming to be adroit for an appearance at one of the big outdoor events. At Grasmere Sports, in 1963, I watched wrestlers emerge from their cocoons of tweed, serge and gabardine to take part in a sport said to have been brought to Lakeland by the Vikings.

The grass in the arena was short and succulent. The ground was firm. I joined the wrestlers in their special enclosure, handy for the rings, noting that some of them were smoking. It was whispered that some had imbibed the stronger forms of liquid refreshment. Yet they were not conspicuously wild or intemperate. One of them told me he was in the twelve-stone class – but was not a natural twelve-stoner. "It means I've got to take weight off. I don't always go into the ring fully fit." A man who had been in competitive wrestling for fifteen years remarked that he had not trained for the past ten years and was now relying on technique. "I'm of pension age – 32 years old."

Cumberland and Westmorland style wrestling seemed a friendly sport. The "ring" was formed of two judges and a referee. I watched two wrestlers shake hands. They greeted each other like long-lost friends. Then the smiles vanished from their faces.

Colourful costume worn by a wrestler.

Each man placed his chin on his opponent's right shoulder and grasped him round the back. The left arm was over the opponent's right and the right arm under the other's left arm. It sounded complicated but, seen at Grasmere Sports, it looked easy and natural.

The men might be experimenting with a new form of dance. In fact, they had "takken 'od", a distinctive feature of this style, which is sometimes known as "back hold wrestling." If one of them were to break the hold before the other has been floored, he would lose the bout. The wrestling officials, kneeling on rubber mats, had a low vantage point from which to keep a sharper eye on the wrestlers' movements. The only illegitimate move in Cumberland & Westmorland style wrestling is – kicking!

Cumberland and Westmorland style wrestling. In his young days, Ransome joined a group of lads who were keen on the sport.

In putting his opponent on the ground, a wrestler might choose from seven or eight different *chips*, or throws. To *hype,* he gets his knee between his opponent's legs and lifts him off the ground, striking his legs outward in the same movement. A refinement of this is known as the *swing hype.* I watched a wrestler actually swinging the luckless opponent round once or twice. He appeared to be helpless during that time.

One of the most famous *chips* is the *cross buttock.* A man puts his buttock quickly under the other man's stomach, uses it as a fulcrum and throws him over his head or shoulder. If it comes off, it is spectacular, and rouses the crowd to applause. If it doesn't come off, the wrestler who tried it is vulnerable to himself being thrown.

Also in Ransome's book *Swallowdale* we read about hound-trailing, about which the author was vague. He referred to the man who laid the scent trail as "a native". He was dragging a "bundle of dusty sacking at the end of a rope." The "sack" as described by Nancy, "is full of some smelly stuff." Naturally, the hounds were allowed to depart at the same time and no one was with them!

Ransome most certainly attended hound trails because his *Swallowdale* account notes that as trail was nearing its end "the whole world was yelling itself hoarse". What was a hound trail really like? At the first hound trail I attended as an emissary of *Cumbria* magazine, my first lesson was to call the contestants hounds, not dogs.

A trail hound seems to me a mournful animal. A slim, lean body is draped by loose skin, almost as if it was wearing a suit a size or two on the big side and was anxious to grow into it. "That hound looks half-starved," I commented at one trail I observed. The owner said: "Appen so, but it eats better than I do. Costs me about £3 a week to keep it in condition." He fed it on whites of eggs – the yolk was considered too good for it – and glucose. This man thought nothing of visiting a butcher's shop for two or three pounds of shin beef for his best animal.

At Kendal, in 1963, I beheld what was up to then the richest hound trail of them all. The prize money was £150, most of it forthcoming from a brewery firm, in whose liquid assets a large crowd was indulging. There were forty-six starters, each of whom had qualified via other trails. The value of this line-up was around £8,000 in flesh and bone alone, quite apart from the large sums at stake via the bookies. A portly man mopped his brow. "This warm weather'll favour t'bitches," he told me.

The owners seemed almost as lish as their charges. I heard that when a hound is in training it is walked between seven and eight miles a day, the time divided between morning and evening. At other times it was firmly kennelled. It was never allowed to run loose. A hound had its last meal twenty-four hours before the race. It would then be perfectly fit, without an ounce of surplus tissue. "Apart from that we don't want a hound stopping at every tree round the course," said another, with great delicacy.

Two lish men laid the trail by dragging a neatly-tied bundle of woollen rags across the ground to determine the precise course the hounds would follow. The rags had been impregnated, by a local chemist, with a mixture of paraffin, aniseed and turpentine. If pure aniseed had been used, a hound's

Herdwick sheep in Patterdale. They occasionally get "cragfast", as described in *Winter Holiday*.

The start of a hound-trail - a traditional Lakeland sport that features in *Swallowdale*.

nose would be so full it would smell the stuff wherever it went. Meeting half way round the course, and heading towards start and end respectively, the trailers worked with precision. A hound trail that lasted for less than 25 minutes or over 45 minutes would be declared void.

As trailers were signalled-in, a silence descended on the field. The white flag was dropped. Hounds raced away, accelerating to well over twenty miles an hour, then settling down to a graceful rhythmic lope that carried them effortlessly on their ten-mile journey, during which a river would be forded and innumerable walls and hedges crossed. Ironically, they would end the course within sight of the place where it had begun.

At the finish, I watched owners open cans containing delicacies for the hounds – raw meat, gingerbread, or anything else favoured by their animals. Towels, cloth, handkerchief were unfurled. A shout went up as the first dog appeared. The line of owners was now a waving, yelling, trembling, demented mob towards which the hounds raced as a tawny, rippling flood, for it was to be a close finish. Across the broad white tape swept the animals, with *Gay Gordon* nicely ahead of *Sunnyside Lad, Jack Pot, Fire Bronze* and *Gazelle*. The timekeeper's watch clicked, fixing the duration of the trail at an acceptable 27 minutes, 5 seconds.

Chapter XI of *Winter Holiday* tells of cragfast sheep, a not unusual occurrence in the Lake District, even though the Herdwick sheep breed was well tuned to the rocky environment. The sheep was seen when the children, having dragged a sledge up a steep fellside, were enacting their version of dog team in High Greenland.

The crossing of a white wilderness was in full swing when the mewing of a buzzard was heard from high crags. Then a faint bleat floated down on the wind from a ledge-bound sheep. How it was rescued, by rope and the steady nerves of the young folk, made for an exciting tale. A reviewer of the book in the *Spectator* described Ransome's tale as "hair-raising, credible and amusing".

With Hugh Walpole

To follow a slender link between Ransome and the northern area of the Lake District, I crossed Dunmail Raise into the Keswick area. Ransome was friendly with the novelist Hugh Walpole who, at the age of forty, had purchased Brackenburn, "a little paradise" near Keswick. Being a newish house overlooking Derwentwater, it appealed to Walpole at first glance. There was no haggling over the price nor did he seek professional advice about its purchase.

Ransome had first met Walpole in 1908 when a dinner was arranged in Soho by Ethel Colburn Mayne. Her aim was to promote Walpole as a novelist. The evening ended when Walpole accompanied Ransome to his home. They chatted until a late hour about their literary aspirations. Ransome was impressed by Walpole's ability to begin a story – and finish it – because at that time his own stories didn't seem to hang together. They subsequently met each other in Russia, falling out over a minor matter, the quarrel being unresolved for sixteen years.

Walpole wrote a complimentary review of Ransome's *Peter Duck* in *The Observer*. Ransome visited him at his new home Brackenburn. Walpole listed some of the attractions in *The Brackenburn Book,* his grand name for his daily journal: "Running stream, garden, lawn, daffodils, squirrels, music-room, garage, four bedrooms, bath – All!"

Walpole shared with Ransome a regard for Collingwood's *Thorstein of the Mere*. In his newspaper review of a reprint of the book in 1929,

which in my copy was pasted on an inner cover, Walpole pronounced Collingwood as King of Lakeland. His book, first published in 1895, had been a constant companion of climbers up the Old Man and Helvellyn, also "to dreamers in Stonethwaite and Newlands, to the friends of Mr Thurnham's bookshop in Carlisle or Mr Chaplin's bookshop in Keswick."

He had first read the book, as a lad of thirteen, when staying in a farmhouse above Wastwater. About the same time he read *Eric Brighteyes* "and for months after, the world was peopled only with Norsemen, and lovely maidens with long, braided yellow hair. Young as Walpole was he realised this difference between the two books, that while in *Eric Brighteyes* the tale was the thing, in *Thorstein* there was something much deeper, the land itself. It is this that gives *Thorstein* its immortality..."

Brackenburn was originally to be "the abode of my old age"; a quiet retreat, where he might work without constant interruption. Walpole spent his last days here and died in 1941, to be interred in the churchyard at St John's, Keswick, where today a Celtic-style cross marks the spot. When, in 1986, I sat in the drawing room at Brackenburn, courtesy of the owners, mulling over the Walpole-Ransome friendship, I had an affinity with an early Lakeland tourist who favoured using a Claude glass, turning his back on the scenery when composing a view that was reflected in the glass. Facing the large fireplace in Brackenburn, I sat with my back to the window,

Brackenburn, overlooking Derwentwater, the home of the
novelist Hugh Walpole, who once wrote: "Arthur Ransome
is the best writer for boys and girls in England today."

yet the lake, the woods and fells were spread before me in panoramic splendour, thanks to an ultra-long mirror that Walpole had installed, at a slight angle, just over the fireplace.

Walpole became a man of two worlds. He had by no means cast off the literary world of London, in which he had been absorbed for years. He might think of himself as a country squire when he was at Brackenburn, and he no doubt sincerely believed when he arrived here from London that this was the most satisfying place in which to be. For a time, he laboured with the pen, and entertained his friends, joining in any local activities that appealed to him. He would then find an excuse to leave for a spell in London.

Rupert Hart-Davis confirmed the impression I had of Walpole as a man who needed each of his worlds. He had been bored if he remained in one of them for too long. Walpole, reviewing *Peter Duck* in *The Observer,* noted: "Arthur Ransome is the best writer for boys and girls in England today. *Peter Duck* [third book in the series] is enchanting. It is so well written that you don't realise that it is written at all. The adventures just seem to occur to oneself."

Sanctuary in Rusland

In 1948, Ransome bought Lowick Hall, two miles west of Spark Bridge, in the valley of the Crake. The property, with an attendant farm, was old, large, much-altered and careworn. Running the place was costly. Arthur and Evgenia stayed there for two years, then scuttled back to London, adopting a routine of summering in Lakeland and wintering in London. *Great Northern?,* the last of the Swallows book, an exciting story set on the island of Lewis in the Outer Hebrides, was published in 1947. By this time, however, Ransome was losing his passion for fiction. His literary endeavours were acknowledged with the award of an honorary doctorate from the University of Leeds and, in 1953, with the presentation of a CBE.

In the summer of 1955, a hankering for the Lake District led to the renting of a dilapidated cottage at Haverthwaite. It offered a splendid view of the Rusland Valley. (The name Rusland was derived from Ranulf's Land and by a curious quirk Ransome's surname came from "Runulf's Son"!). Bird life in the valley was profuse. The mewing of a circling buzzard might break the stillness. Red deer inhabited Rusland Moss; it was here that hinds dropped their calves. During the autumnal rut, incoming stags – the finest free-ranging stags in Lakeland – made the evening air shiver with their roaring. It was a sound that did not have a special appeal for the Ransomes, who wintered in London.

For almost the whole of 1959, Ransome, aged 74, was bedridden at his Putney home, being visited regularly by Hart-Davis, his literary executor designate. Now and again he dined at their home. In *The Lyttelton Hart-Davis,* in which I was especially interested, having chatted with Hart-Davis at his Yorkshire fireside, I read of Arthur's bad back, the start of a long and painful run of a form of rheumatoid arthritis. After lunch, those present would gather round his bed. When the "poor old boy" had lain a-bed for four months, he was – according to Hart-Davis – bored stiff, unable to sleep, often in pain. In June that year, he had a spell in hospital. Yet by September, he was at home, much improved and able to totter into the dining room on two sticks. Ransome had been bedfast since Christmas.

In 1960, the Ransomes bought Hill Top, which was a Haverthwaite holiday cottage they had rented. It was intended for permanent residence. Arthur had spells of ill-health, also some "bad tumbles", in one of which his spectacles, a vital accessory, were badly damaged. When Ernest Altounyan died in 1962, *The Times* in its obituary referred to the children as being models for the *Swallows* and Ernest playing a part in devising the books. This led the crusty Ransome to omit from his autobiography mention of the Altounyan children, who had crewed the *Swallow.* He had begun to write this work but died before its completion. Hart-Davis, after writing a prologue and epilogue, published the autobiography in 1976.

Sir Rupert Hart-Davis, aware that the ageing, doddery Arthur could scarcely move, gave him a

Arthur Ransome and Evgenia in later years. (Brotherton Library, University of Leeds)

The impressive sight of a red deer roaring, photographed at Lowther.

special treat. In the summer of 1960 he arranged a car trip taking in some of his old fishing haunts. Arthur, so weak he was unable to get out of the car, was driven to within a short distance of the rivers he knew in fine detail. In his later years, Arthur was ever dependent on Evgenia. He did not always find it possible to cope with her moods. She had times of ill-health, suffering from sciatica and having two heart attacks. She had an uncanny insight into what small boys were fond of to eat and met that demand with chocolate fingers. When, in Arthur's latter days, Charles Lupton, aged nine, was ushered into his presence, the lad was rewarded with the gift of – a blue paper clip!

An aged Ransome was delighted when told that Hart-Davis was to retire from publishing (he and his wife would settle in a grand house, formerly a parsonage, in the valley of the Swale). By 1964, the bounds of his physical world had shrunk to within the walls of a room on the upper floor of their Lakeland home. In the autumn of the following year, after experiencing two mild heart attacks, the devoted Evgenia regretfully switched the care of Arthur to hospital nurses. He died in Cheadle Royal Hospital near Manchester on June 3, 1967, aged 83 years. (Evgenia, his long-term wife, who had given him support while being a stern critic of his literary work, arranged for her name to be put on the simple tombstone at Rusland churchyard while she was still alive. She was, indeed, to live for a further eight years).

A memorial service for Arthur Ransome took place at St Martin-in-the-Fields, London. Hart-Davis, in his address, observed that he would be assured of exactly the kind of immortality he would have chosen – "the voices of generation after generation of children, delightedly asking their parents: Is it real?" Rupert Hart-Davis played a notable part in the later years. He had long since left Jonathan Cape to start his own publishing business. Indeed, when this happened, Ransome had purchased some shares in the company.

Arthur and Evgenia were interred in an idyllic setting, this being the churchyard at St Paul's Church, Rusland, several miles from his beloved Coniston Water. Arthur had first glimpsed the church in 1956, when – during a summer holiday at a house near the Rusland beeches – he bestrode the banks of Ashes Beck, which loses its identity in the

St Paul's, Rusland, where both Arthur and Evgenia
Ransome were interred in the peaceful churchyard.

stream flowing down to Rusland Pool. Entranced by the church's location, and revelling it its peacefulness, he mentioned to the Rev J S Boulter, vicar, that he would like to be buried in the churchyard, close to a Corsican pine, whose needles would be gently strummed by a breeze.

On a July day, anxious to enjoy the "feel" of Arthur Ransome Country, I visited this last resting place. Stormy weather had moderated by the time I parked my car in the old familiar surroundings of Hay Bridge – a nature reserve founded and sustained for many years by Helen (Tissie) Fooks. An American lady, she invited me to serve on the committee. I had met Herbert Fooks, her husband, on a visit in the 1960s. Herbie, as she tended to call him, had been a former keeper of the royal waterfowl at St James's Park, London. Now and again, when the larder was almost bare, he had done some surreptitious culling of ducks!

He and Tissie moved to the Lake District in 1958 on his appointment by the Forestry Commission as their first game warden. (Herbie was a man after Arthur Ransome's heart, being solitary, obsessed with nature, cosmopolitan and, latterly, rooted in the Lake District. Herbie died in 1968 and three years later the estate became a nature reserve, dedicated to his memory). I felt as much at home in Rusland Valley as Ransome would have done. Here was a backwater in a busy world where the days were punctuated by the mewing of buzzard and, in autumn, the roaring of red stags. The road from Bouth to Hay Bridge has none of the devil-may-care attitude of a modern highway. The people who had used it for many years were farmfolk, tending their Shorthorn cattle and Herdwick sheep.

I had attended meetings in the home of the Fooks, which was a large converted barn. Above a gaping fireplace was the head of a moose and its beady eyes seemed to follow me as I walked around the room! From my seat near a huge window, I switched my attention to a red squirrel or to the sparrow hawk that preyed on Tissie's stock of ornamental doves, taking at least one a day. A balcony was of generous size, like the bridge of a small coaster. From it, I viewed an enclosed stock of fallow deer and a testy roebuck that Tissie fed daily, keeping an eye on horns as sharp and rigid as coat-hooks. Beyond, free-ranging roe flit like grey shadows through former coppice woods and wandered about the mossland at last light. Sanctuary had been set apart for woodland red deer – among the finest free-ranging "reds" in the land. Their ancestors had roamed the hills and valleys of High Furness since time immemorial.

I stood in silence beside a stone memorial to Tissie and recalled when I last visited her. It was on an autumn evening. I was motoring home after spending the day among the folk of the Duddon Valley. By the time I reached Hay Bridge, via road and track that had an aversion to going straight, it was dusk. With no white lines on the track to the house I motored cautiously. The captive deer were like shadows. A tawny owl was hooting. Tissie offered me a cup of coffee. While she was making it, I listened to the distinctive crackle of a wood fire and came under the beady scrutiny of the stuffed moose!

Hay Bridge was not intended to be a zoo. A few animals were enclosed because otherwise they would have been destroyed or, even worse, demoralised after being mollycoddled by humans, turned out into the wild. What does one do with a roe kid whose mother was shot by poachers? Or a kid found on the main road to Windermere, its parents chased off by dogs? Or a deserted red calf picked up by Yorkshire holidaymakers in the Highlands, taken home as a pet and, within a few weeks, attaining a huge size and rampaging nature?

My walk to the last resting-place of Arthur Ransome began with a path leading to Rusland Moss, where my feet created a drummy sound on a boardwalk. Around me – but not in sight, skulking in a huge tract of soggy woodland – were an estimated eighty expectant red deer hinds. One or two had already dropped their calves. In September, stags would move into the area to cover the hinds. The Moss was bird-busy with siskin, reed bunting, sedge warbler, great spotted woodpecker, robin and wren. A newly-fledged family of wrens - second or maybe even third brood – clung to trees or flew to where mum was feeding them with insects. Florally, there were fine specimens of bog asphodel, purple loosestrife and bell heather.

Breaking tree cover, I entered countryside well-known to Ransome. Here were fields of tousled vegetation. A venerable little bridge spanned a river where, it was said, he enjoyed fishing. The path was linked with a narrow road. I followed it, between hedges and beside white-painted dwellings, until I had a picture-postcard impression of the enchanting Rusland Church – light grey in tone and perched high, as though it might be half-way to heaven. The motor road, steep and narrow, passes the church. I preferred the steep footpath leading to a sheep-proof gate in a wall and the churchyard.

Arthur and Evgenia's grave was not ostentatious, being a simply-engraved stone slab. I pondered on the Leeds lad who enjoyed family holidays by Coniston Water, who chatted with charcoal burners and – in love with Lakeland - wrote the enduringly attractive book *Swallows and Amazons*, a children's adventure story he could not help writing. "It almost wrote itself." It became a popular work with children the world over. Within the church was an Arthur Ransome corner, with texts and pictures relating to the great man. Arthur Ransome had died peacefully, as people do when confined to a wheelchair and suffering from memory loss. It's the onlookers who are ill-at-ease. He died in a hospital outside Manchester. His enchanting books keep alive our memories of him and the Lakeland life so vastly different from the one he knew.

Ransome will long be remembered for his literary achievements in the period from 1932 until 1947. He had spells of debilitating illness and, restlessly, had frequent changes of address, yet once he had set the style for his children's books he produced them with awesome rapidity. Each appeared on the bookstalls within a month or two of its completion. As a fellow author, I was impressed – and amused – when I read that if necessary Ransome would correct the proofs of a book at the printer's. (Now it's done by email!).

The simple stone slab in Rusland churchyard that marks the last resting place of Arthur and Evgenia.

Ransome's Lakeland Books

Swallows and Amazons (1930)

This is the first of what was to become known as the *Swallows and Amazons* series, involving children with a taste for adventure. It was inspired by experiences in August 1929. (As related earlier, Ransome wrote this book speedily following a gift from the about-to-depart Altounyans of a pair of Turkish slippers. The first lines were typed on March 24; he had just resigned as a journalist on the *Manchester Guardian*). The first edition dust jacket of the book had the title and a make-belief map, drawn by Steven Spurrier. It proved irresistible to children with a sense of adventure.

The surname Walker was chosen by Ransome for the crew of the *Swallow* – Tanqui (re-named John, to give the craft a male captain), Susan (mate), Titty (coyly referred to in places as Kitty; real name Mavis; able seaman) and Roger (ship's boy). The family were holidaymaking at Holly Howe, a lakeside farmhouse. While staying at a farm, the Walkers were permitted by their father, a naval officer in Malta, to sail to and camp on Wild Cat Island.

The *Amazon* was manned by Nancy Blackett and her younger sister, Peggy, who lived at Beckfoot, near the head of Coniston Water. They claimed ownership of Wild Cat Island. Nancy, who captained the boat, became Ruth in the story. Peggy, the mate, assumed the name Margaret. They classified themselves as pirates and, using the sailing dinghy which in real life is called *Mavis,* flew the skull and crossbones. They made a surprise attack on the Walker camp. At first, it was war. Then peace as they joined forces against the Blacketts' Uncle Jim, dubbed Captain Flint after the character in *Treasure Island.* He shared the occupancy of a houseboat with a parrot, known – unsurprisingly – as Polly.

Alone on a boat at night, Titty eavesdropped on some thieves who were burying on an islet the old chest belonging to Uncle Jim which they had filched from the houseboat. The chest contained treasures, mainly of a literary kind. It was duly re-united with its owner, to mutual satisfaction. Uncle Jim, who had affinities with Ransome himself, was made to walk the plank. There followed affable talk and refreshments. Polly the parrot was given to Titty. A storm swept the lake. After coping with it, the Swallows and Amazons became landlubbers once again, preparing for a new year at school. They promised each other that next year they would meet again...

Swallowdale (1931)

A year has elapsed. The Swallows sailed towards Wild Cat Island. They had in mind another meeting with the Amazons and a renewal of their friendship with Captain Flint. Enter Maria Turner, Great Aunt of the Blacketts, temporarily ensconced at Beckfoot, their home. The girls managed to escape her attention, arranging a rendezvous with the Swallows. Unhappily, John wrecked *Swallow* on Pike Rock near Horseshoe Cove. Plans to visit the island were thus in abeyance.

Titty and Roger discovered Swallowdale, a secret valley tucked away at a much higher elevation than the lake. As repair work on *Swallow* proceeded, the Swallows camped, fished and met local farmers at a time when a hound trail was being organised. The Amazons had been left to the attention of their formidable Great Aunt. Towards the end of her stay, the Amazons planned an expedition with the Swallows – to trek to Amazon Valley and climb the formidable Kanchenjunga (Coniston Old Man).

Mist shrouded the fells. Titty and Roger lost their way. Roger, spraining his ankle, was saved and lodged at the home of a veteran charcoal-burner. With *Swallow* available once again after repairs, Swallows and Amazons organised a race to Beckfoot from a starting point at the houseboat belonging to Captain Flint. A feast followed. The children achieved their ambition to re-visit Wild Cat Island.

Winter Holiday (1933)

Fourth book in the series (the third was *Peter Duck*, set outside the Lake District). Ransome's main inspiration was school-day memories of Windermere during the Great Frost of 1895. We are introduced to the Ds (Dick and Dorothea Callum), who are having a winter holiday at Dixon's Farm, on the shore of Coniston Water. They have sailing to Wild Cat Island in view. The Swallows and Amazons, staying at the usual native settlements (Holly Howe and Beckfoot), were contacted by the Ds, who had built an igloo and were planning an expedition to the North Pole.

An igloo was built in the woodland above Holly Howe. Arctic conditions arrived. The Ds arranged to join the expedition. The holiday was extended after Nancy suffered from mumps and the others were in quarantine. When Captain Flint's houseboat was icebound with the freezing over of the lake, it was re-named *Fram*. It was from here that the polar expedition took place. (Ransome was familiar with the name Fridtjof Nansen, the outstanding Norwegian explorer, with whom he had spent an afternoon by the Gulf of Riga during a sojourn in the Baltic in 1921).

The Ds, confused by a signal from Beckfoot, were lost in a blizzard. A relief expedition of Swallows and Amazons headed towards the North Pole in the Arctic night.

Pigeon Post (1936)

For once, the children did not go sailing. Hearing from Slater Bob, an old slate miner, of a lost gold seam on the fells, they encamped at Tyson's Farm, thence to the High Topps. Captain Flint was said to be prospecting for gold in South America. They had the company of the Ds once again and Squashy Hat, a memorable new character, who was also prospecting.

The pigeons (of the title) were used for sending daily messages between the team and their base at Beckfoot. As Nancy remarked: "A pigeon a day keeps the natives away." The children discovered a cave fashioned by old-time miners. It contains a rich vein of copper, which they had initially taken to be gold. Meanwhile, a message from Titty by pigeon post reports the outbreak of fire on the Topps. It is duly extinguished. Captain Flint reveals it was the prospect of finding copper, not gold, that had taken him to South America.

The Picts and the Martyrs (1943)

This book was written during the Second World War, when the Ransomes were living at the Heald, beside Coniston Water. Their boat *Coch-y-bonddhu* was a conspicuous feature on the lake. The book, the last of the Lake books, dedicated to Ransome's Aunt Helen, features the Blackett sisters (Amazons, martyrs to the other Great Aunt) and the Ds (Dick and Dorothea, who become Picts with a woodland base).

The summer holiday had begun. Captain Flint and Mrs Blackett were on a voyage during which, hopefully, she would recover from a severe attack of flu. She invited Dick and Dorothea to stay with her daughters. The cook at Beckfoot would keep an eye on them. Plans for a house party were changed when Great Aunt Maria arrives and takes charge.

In order to keep their identity from Great Aunt, the Ds became Picts, their temporary home being a woodland hut above Beckfoot. The Amazons, as Martyrs, appeased Great Aunt, so she would not be angry with mother. A sailing dinghy, named *Scarab,* belonging to the Ds, was a newcomer in the Ransome saga. Events become complex and the children keep from Great Aunt the presence of visitors at the house.

Also by W.R. Mitchell, available from Great Northern Books:

HANNAH HAUXWELL – 80 Years in the Dales

THUNDER IN THE MOUNTAINS – The Men Who Built Ribblehead

WAINWRIGHT – His life from Milltown to Mountain

BEATRIX POTTER – Her Lakeland Years

HERRIOT – A Vet's Life

www.greatnorthernbooks.co.uk